WHY NO MONEY DOWN REAL ESTATE REALLY DOES WORK

WHY NO MONEY DOWN REAL ESTATE REALLY DOES WORK

RON SEARCY
Author of *Divorced In The Courthouse, But Not In Heaven*
and *How Anyone Can Understand The Bible*

iUniverse, Inc.
New York Lincoln Shanghai

WHY NO MONEY DOWN REAL ESTATE REALLY DOES WORK

iUniverse books may be ordered through booksellers or by contacting:

iUniverse
2021 Pine Lake Road, Suite 100
Lincoln, NE 68512
www.iuniverse.com
1-800-Authors (1-800-288-4677)

ISBN-13: 978-0-595-42743-7 (pbk)
ISBN-13: 978-0-595-68138-9 (cloth)
ISBN-13: 978-0-595-87074-5 (ebk)
ISBN-10: 0-595-42743-X (pbk)
ISBN-10: 0-595-68138-7 (cloth)
ISBN-10: 0-595-87074-0 (ebk)

Printed in the United States of America

Dedication

To my sister Rita. Sis, I dedicated this book to you because, you have always been there for me when I needed you and especially, during the rough times in my life. Though, we have had our strong differences in opinion, we always revert back to what's really important in life, our family and loving one another.

I wish you the utmost success in your new career in real estate and hopefully, something that I said in this book will help you to be more successful.

I love you very much.

Contents

Preface

I wrote this book for those that have an interest in real estate and hopefully, this book will open your eyes to non-traditional ways and means of buying and selling real estate that will put more cash in your pocket.

As you will see, most of us get stuck in tradition and we follow what the norm is considered to be without ever opening our eyes to see the vast opportunities in front of us that, we cannot see until someone points them out. That is exactly what I tried to do in this book.

For those of you who may currently hold a real estate license, I hope this book will give you a different insight to the many ways that, you can come up with to close the deal.

One thing for sure, the good Lord is not making any more real estate and the population on planet Earth continues to grow therefore, the price of real estate will keep going up and the demand for it gets greater month-by-month. On one recent reality TV show, most of the people that did not have a college education were involved in real estate one way or another and all were making very high incomes. So, for those of you who did not or cannot attend college, real estate presents an enormous opportunity for you to be wealthy.

Chapter 1

Solving Problems

I want to warn you ahead of time that, almost any licensed realtor that you may approach with the idea of purchasing real estate with no money down will get a very negative result. In fact, they will probably think that you're crazy.

I certainly do not mean any disrespect to any licensed realtor because, I'm very aware of the long, hard hours that they put in but, they have a certain mind set and are taught a certain way as discussed in the previous chapter and basically have their minds closed to this approach.

From what I have seen of the real estate test in my state, anyone with a high school diploma or less can pass the real estate exam. This does not make a person a realtor.

Anyone with $300.00 can get a very nice business suit, male or female, dress the part but, that does not make them a realtor.

I can become an associate with any major real estate firm after receiving my license and dressing the part, contact all of my family and friends and make them aware that, I am licensed and sit in the office and wait for the phone to ring but, that still does not make me a realtor.

What I am getting at is, this is the typical approach that most people have after getting their real estate license and they try to find someone that has enough down payments in order to make a sale.

If, real estate people would just open their minds and look at themselves as problem solvers instead of realtors every day that they come to work, they would sell a lot more real estate.

Someone once said that, you can get anything in life that you want if, you help enough other people get what they want first so, what does the seller of a piece of property want? They want a fair market value for their property and they want their equity out. What's the buyer's problem? Down payment!

You see, in order for the seller to get what they want, they are going to have to help the buyer, in most cases, solve their problem and as always, that is the down payment.

As I stated in the previous chapter to one realtor, if you think that sellers will not sell their property for no money down or, a deal can be worked towards that end, then, I say to you, that's because you never asked and I might add never gave thought to working a deal where both parties will get what they want.

Before I began writing books, I ran a construction company that did repair work on insurance claims for 30 years and in 1996, I put my son-in-law in the business in a rural area of Northwest, Tennessee and not long after he started, a house down the street from him was damaged by fire and smoke.

My son-in-law called me very excited about the opportunity to write an estimate on this damage and the possibility of getting the job. Needless to say, at this point, he was about to starve to death due to the lack of work because, getting in with the insurance companies and proving your credibility is very difficult.

When I saw the house, I told my son-in-law not to get too excited because, he probably would not get the job. Needless to say, this certainly dampened his spirits and he asked why I had said that. I replied that, there was a for sale sign in the yard and that meant that the people did not want the house.

We wrote an estimate for repairs to the property in the amount of $56,000.00 and submitted it to the home owner's insurance company. My son-in-law was very aggressive and was determined to get the job and so, he went by the home owner's place of work on several occasions and finally after several weeks, my son-in-law called me one night and stated that the people wanted to know if, his father-in-law, which of course, is me, would like to buy the property as it was.

I asked my son-in-law if, I understood correctly that, the property was setting on two lots and he affirmed that it was and since this property was at a major lake, I asked him to call a neighbor that had been there for several years, to find out what the value of the two lots were.

My son-in-law called me back and stated that each lot was worth $8,000.00 so, I told my son-in-law that, when a person sells a piece of property, it is their property and they need to set a price and when someone forces me to price their property then, the first thing that I'm going to do is insult them so, I instructed my son-in-law to call the home owner back and tell him that I would give $20,000.00 for the property as it was. My son-in-law reacted immediately and told me that he couldn't do that because, that would make the home owner mad. I told my son-in-law I didn't care if, he did get mad that, and I was going to show him how I purchased real estate and vehicles at such cheap prices.

Within about 20 minutes, my son-in-law called me back in utter amazement that the home owner had agreed to my $20,000.00 offer.

I then went to a local bank with a copy of the estimate of repairs and was able to borrow $40,000.00 against the property. I took $20,000.00 of the $40,000.00 and paid the owner for the property. I then took the other $20,000.00 and had my workers to go in and repair the fire damage. About the time that I got through with the repairs, my youngest daughter that, lived about an hour away was visiting her sister and saw the property and begged old soft-hearted dad to let her move in the house and so I put additional cabinets, dishwasher, and some other things that she wanted changed that cost me an additional $3,000.00 out of my pocket.

The property that I gave $40,000.00 for plus $3,000.00 out of my pocket now appraised at $78,000.00 so, for those who say that you cannot purchase property for no money down, do not know what they are talking about.

Because of its location at a major lake, my guess is that, this property that I still own as I write this book, would appraise for approximately $90,000.00.

There are not too many homes that are on the market where the seller doesn't have at least $5,000.00 to $10,000 in equity and that's after the seller has agreed to pay the closing cost. Now, to you as a real estate investor or to realtors and associate realtors that will read this book, I ask you, how many people do you know in America that are in their early 20's to mid 40's that has that kind of money lying around in a bank account? I don't know about you but, I don't know of any.

What I'm trying to get across to all parties is to stop being brain washed by the old traditional system and come up with creative financing techniques that will sell this piece of property or, if, you are an investor, that will allow you to purchase this piece of property and yes, for little or no money down.

Several years ago, my company was doing a fire damage repair job in a city about 30 miles east of where I live and down the street, there was a house for sell and I could tell by the fact that the yard was grown up that this seller would like very much to get rid of this piece of property.

I contacted the seller and found out that this was a rental property as I had already assumed that it was.

This was a period of time when the interest rates for CD's at the bank were less than four per cent and I offered to purchase the property for no money down and was rejected.

I then asked the seller what he normally rented the property for and he replied that he got $550.00 in advance for the first month and he also got $550.00 for the last month and usually rented the property on a month to month basis.

I then asked the seller what he was going to do with the money after he sold the property. The seller replied that he would probably put the money on CD's and asked me why I wanted to know. I then pulled out a compound interest chart out of my brief case and showed him the tens of thousands of dollars more that he would make over the 30-year period of the mortgage if, he carried the note and I paid 10% than he would if, he put it on CD's.

I then made a second offer by telling the seller that I would give him $1,100.00 down payment and him carry the note at ten per cent interest for a 30-year period and explained to him that, that way it would be the same as renting the property as far as money received and that, I would give him a quit claim deed to be retained by his attorney in the event that I did not make the payments. Therefore, all he had to do was file the quit claim deed and he would not lose any more with me than he would as if, he had rented the property, but on the other hand, he had tens of thousands of dollars to gain by selling me the property this way. This is how I bought this piece of property for very little down.

Unless, you can come up with a "pet rock" idea, there are no get rich quick deals in America. It takes time for money to work for you. However, the real estate business is one of the most lucrative fields that you could possibly get into because there is no more land being made, but there certainly is a lot more people being made that will want to occupy the land. Therefore, even though there may be a few slack times here and there in the real estate field, property will keep increasing in value and using a chosen plan, you can absolutely get filthy rich in this field.

A little simple know how can also allow you to have an extreme high income upon retirement without paying little or nothing in income tax. So, you think I'm crazy, huh? Well, let's see.

The whole idea is to stay as far in debt as possible with safety. That means, in case one of your renters or your buyers skip out on you then, you need to have enough cash set aside to be able to make two or three payments just in case they do not pay you. Another thing that you want to always remember is to use as little of your cash as possible.

Let's say, for instance, that you are in your early to mid 20's as you read this book and over the next 20 years, you purchase at least two pieces of property per year over the next 20 years, so at age 40 to 45, you will own 40 pieces of property.

Next, assuming that property continues to double in value approximately every seven years the first house that you bought for $100,000.00 is now worth $200,000.00 or more. During this period of time, you have always had a renter in the property making the payments for you and the payments were large enough to take care of your insurance and maintenance. Therefore, you really haven't been out anything at all.

Let's say at age 45, you decide you are going to retire so, you go back to the first house that you bought. You get the house refinanced. You borrow 80% of the value of the property and let's just say that the house did not increase as much as you had anticipated. Let's say the house is now worth $150,000. You go to the bank and get a 80% loan, which would be $120,000. Now remember, the house has been paid off during this period of time so, you put $120,000 in your pocket, you still have a renter in the property making your payments for you and the $120,000 that you put in your pocket is completely tax free because, it is a loan.

The next year, you go to house number two that you purchased years ago and do the same thing or, you could do two or three a year if you had 40 houses by the time you are 40 or 45 years old so, the more houses you have, the higher the income that you would have each year by duplicating this on an annual basis.

I'm not smart enough to do all that. Oh, yes, you are! The Lord did not see fit to bless me with a lot of book sense, but he gave me a whole lot of common sense. True story, I had to go to summer school to get out of high school, if that makes you feel any better about yourself.

There is nothing in this book that is above the eighth grade level; however, there is a whole lot to learn and as with anything, it takes hard work and a lot of time.

The fact that nearly 97% of all Americans age 65 and older retire in poverty should not only scare you to death, it should tell you something. It tells me that if, I work for somebody else, there's a very good chance that when I retire, I will be flat broke.

You see, in the game of life, you're going to work hard somewhere all of your life so, the question is, are you getting paid what you think you're worth?

Also, in the game of life, as to your career, if, you work for yourself, you have two choices. For instance, I could go get my carpenter belt and paint brush back out and I could make a much better than average living. However, there's only so many hours in a day, so many days in a week therefore, my income is limited so, the secret to becoming wealthy is to have a lot of other people working for you and making a little off of a lot of different people.

Someone once said that, you can get anything in life that you want if, you help enough other people get what they want first.

This certainly applies to the real estate business. The seller can get what they want if, they help the buyer get what they want first and of course, that is the down payment. You need to approach the real estate business of buying, selling, and investing as a problem solver. The seller has a problem and so do you so, if, you will help the seller solve his problem by presenting dozens and dozens and dozens of offers until, you find one that will work then, you have a deal and both of you are happy.

As to education, I try to put this book on a eighth to tenth grade level where, any person that has a burning desire to succeed can do so in this field by simply learning a few techniques. However, I do suggest that for knowledge sake, you attend real estate school and I will leave it up to you whether you decide you want to take the test or not. Personally, I would prefer just to have the knowledge as I did in taking property and casualty school classes without taking the test since that was related to two fields that I have worked in the last 30 years being, an independent home owners' claims adjuster and also a general contractor doing repair work for insurance companies.

If, you still doubt whether you're smart enough, please give some consideration to the fact that handicapped people, uneducated people, and people from other countries have come to America and all have become millionaires and we all have heard stories of these people so, the question is, if, they can do it, what makes you think that you can't? You see, when you have a free-enterprise system such as we do in America and you have a burning desire to succeed, you're willing to pay the price or in other words, willing to put in long, hard hours at the beginning in order to reap the rewards later, the only thing that's keeping you from getting there is, the right vehicle to take you there. It may be computers, the construction business, writing a book, real estate, or hundreds of other avenues so, the only thing lacking is, for you to find your niche, and apply your ability. It may not be the real estate business so, try many different things as, I much rather try and fail than not try at all.

<u>NOTES</u>

_____

_____

_____

_____

_____

_____

_____

_____

_____

_____

_____

_____

_____

_____

_____

_____

_____

NOTES

_____

_____

_____

_____

_____

_____

_____

_____

_____

_____

_____

_____

_____

_____

_____

_____

<u>NOTES</u>

_____

_____

_____

_____

_____

_____

_____

_____

_____

_____

_____

_____

_____

_____

_____

<u>NOTES</u>

Chapter 2

How Money Works

In this chapter, you will begin to understand why I have said that nearly 97% of all Americans age 65 and older retire in poverty.

The reason they do is, they do not understand how money works and specifically, how compound interest works. I want you to see how it works and once aware, you can use compound interest to your advantage instead of letting credit card companies and banks use it against you. The average person wastes thousands of dollars on interest.

In the first part, I'm going to show you why you want to purchase real estate with little or no money down and why, once understood, there can be unbelievable long-term results.

I have personally showed this to many realtors and was received by every one of them in absolute shock and wonderment of why this is not taught in any of their classes that they have taken, including advanced classes.

Most people fail to understand rate of return because, they confuse cash flow with, "making something on their money". They can't see their wealth building so, they think that they are not making anything.

In real estate, rate of return means the total amount earned and it includes but, not limited to cash flow. Some of your wealth may, for a short time, be invisible because, you don't actually have the green stuff in your hands. The amount of your rental income, after expenses, is your cash flow. This, however, is only part of your return for the year.

As I previously said, there are unbelievable long-term profits you can make as a real estate investor but, you must first understand how this comes about.

Your rate of return equals money made, divided by money invested if, you wanted to put it into a mathematical formula.

Money invested is a down payment and the closing cost if, you have to pay any of it.

Money made is a bit more complicated because; it is made of four different things:

1. Appreciation: This is how much the property's value has risen since you first purchased it.

2. Equity build up: As each payment is made, part of the principle is then paid down and this creates your equity in the property.

3. Tax savings: This is in the form of depreciation. In other words, its money you would have paid to the IRS, but because of the depreciation tax laws, you get to keep it.

4. Cash flow: This is your net cash from rent you collect after you deduct all of your expenses each month.

Rate of return is:

Depreciation + equity build up + tax savings + cash flow

(divided by)

Money invested

Next, you need to learn how to calculate the rate of return so that you can find out whether you are making any money on your property or not.

Let's say, for example purposes, you own a $100,000.00 rental house. The lot it is on is not depreciable, but is worth $20,000. Let's also say that you bought it with a $20,000 down payment.

You are renting it for $1,600 a month, but your mortgage payments are $800 a month and the upkeep and other costs average to be $800 a month, so your cash flow is zero. This is why people think they are not earning anything on their investment.

Let's say, for example purposes, that the rental house appreciates in value 10% per year. This isn't money in your pocket until you sell or refinance, but it is still part of your net worth when taking into account how your investment is doing. Let's figure it at $10,000.00 in this example.

The equity in our example was built up by two-and-a-half per cent this year, so two-and-a-half per cent of $80,000.00 (value of the house) amounts to $2,000.00.

Under the 1986 Tax Reform Act, it allows 27.5-year straight line depreciation on residential property up to a maximum of $25,000.00 for those individuals actually involved with their properties. In our example, divide the $80,000.00 rental property value by 27.5. This calculates depreciation in our example to be $2,909.00.

Let's further assume you're in the maximum tax bracket of 28%. Your tax savings would be $814.00. Any tax savings is really an addition to your cash flow since taxes saved can be spent now.

We now have all the factors in your rate of return, so let's see how well you're doing.

Your rate of return = $10,000.00 appreciation + $2,000.00 equity build up + $840.00 tax savings + 0 cash flow, divided by $20,000.00 invested cash total, we have:

$$\frac{\$10,000.00 + \$2,000.00 + \$814.00 + 0 = 64\%}{\text{Rate of Return} = \$20,000.00}$$

Note: All of the factors add up to $12,814 that is on the top line, so your figures are:

$$\frac{\$12,814.00}{\$20,000.00} = 64\%$$

Now, you will begin to see why you want to make as small a down payment or purchase property with no money down.

If, you can make a smaller down payment without raising the monthly payment, look what happens:

For $10,000.00 down, rate of return = $12,814.00
$$\frac{\text{For \$10,000.00 down, rate of return} = \$12,814.00}{\$10,000.00} = 128\%$$

$$\frac{\text{For \$5,000 down, rate of return} = \$12,814.00}{\$5,000.00} = 256\%$$

$$\frac{\text{For \$1,000 down, rate of return} = \$12,814.00}{\$1,000.00} = 1281\%$$

This is the miracle of a term called leverage. The smaller your down payment, the bigger return on your invested dollar. You simply get richer faster and this is why you want to find motivated sellers who are willing to sit down and listen to different proposals.

As a real estate investor, you must also learn how to calculate the percentage of your investment yield. Put in simple terms, your rate of return is the increase in value of your real estate divided by the down payment. For investors, this again shows why you want to buy for little or no down payment.

Let's say for example, a property increases in value $10,000.00 and you pay $20,000.00 down:

$$\frac{\$10,000.00 \text{ increase}}{\$20,000.00 \text{ down payment}} = 50\% \text{ pay back on cash invested}$$

$$\frac{\$10,000.00 \text{ increase}}{\$10,000.00 \text{ down payment}} = 100\% \text{ pay back on cash invested}$$

$$\frac{\$10,000.00 \text{ increase}}{\$1,000.00 \text{ down payment}} = 1,000\% \text{ pay back on cash invested}$$

I have mentioned previously that, nearly 97% of all Americans age 65 and older retire in poverty yet, we are in the richest country in the world, and so what's the problem?

Americans save less than anyone else in the free world, but that's not really the problem because, they would save more if, they had any idea about how compound interest works.

For most Americans, they have done what mom and dads did, as far as investing and saving their money and have used banks and insurance companies, mainly life insurance policies.

This is the "brainwashing" process I have constantly talked about realizing that, most children follow in the steps of what their mother and dad did. You see, when the interest rate you're getting on your money does not exceed the rate of inflation then, you're not making anything because, and inflation is eating up the buying power that is being earned.

For instance, if your saving account is paying 4% on your money, and this year's rate of inflation is 4%, then you have made nothing.

If, you want to obtain wealth, don't do it with a life insurance policy, as what you see is not what you get.

When you purchase a life insurance policy that, has a so called savings with it, no matter what the insurance companies may call it, it is still the same thing. Basically it's living and dying at the same time, so, unless you can figure out how to both at one time, that is a flawed concept.

The sales pitch that you will receive from an insurance agent will be in the form of a fancy computer print-out showing what they are presently paying percentage wise and impress you with all this money you will have at retirement, is absolute bologna.

In many cases, it's not what you've been told that is important; it's what you haven't been told. Let me tell you what they don't tell you.

They don't tell you that the 9, 10, or 11 percent rate of return that, they are going to give you, is before they deduct the cost of insurance, policy fees and other charges. The real rate of return is less than 5%, and in most cases, you will be just as well of putting your money in the bank.

No matter what an insurance company calls most of these new policies, it usually is still a universal life policy, and unless the agent checks option B, in which case, if, they do, the agent, will earn less commission. Almost every policy that, I've personally seen has option A, or something similar to that, like, option one and option two which means that when you die, the life insurance company will pay your family only the face value of the policy and the insurance company keeps all the so called savings (cash value).

If, you have any doubt as far as to what I am saying, contact your state insurance commissioners office and ask them and they will tell you that the cash value on a life insurance policy belongs to insurance company otherwise, why do you think you have to borrow your own money if, you wanted a policy loan?

The question is, would you do business with a bank if, your savings account worked like that?

It just makes sense to treat your life insurance as if, it were your homeowners or auto insurance, you want the proper coverage with a good company, and you want the best price available.

You can do this by purchasing the cheapest term insurance that, you can find and with the Internet access today, you can find a good level 20-year policy that, will give you the coverage that you need. This will save you a great deal in premium money per month.

Next, separate your savings from your insurance. That way, if you die, you're spouse gets both the savings and the insurance proceeds.

For those of you that do decide real estate investing is not for you or if, you intended to and just never got started, setting aside just a little a month into a good performing mutual fund will give you a considerable retirement fund if, you have enough years to do the savings.

For those of you like me, the Lord did not bless me with a lot of book sense, but he gave me a bushel basket of common sense. If, you had a license security agent come to your home, if you're like me you'd be more confused when they left than, before they came.

They will use terminology, graphs, charts and other things that will thoroughly confuse you. I am going to put this in common sense language and explain to you how mutual funds work.

Let's say that Joe John came up with a pet pig idea and was selling pet pigs by the millions and was on the New York stock exchange, and you decide to get in on the wealth that is being created and invest a half million dollars of which, you just inherited.

The last thing in the world that you expect to happen was, the pet pig disease got into the herd and all the pigs died. Therefore, you had all your money in one basket, so to speak, and just lost your half million.

Lets say that you did inherit a half million dollars and you went out on your own on the New York stock exchange and invested a portion of your money in several different corporations that are well known. Therefore, you spread your money around realizing that each year, some stocks will gain while others lose but, you ride it out for a 20 year period. More than likely, you will be very wealthy.

Mutual funds work something like this except, it allows those with small investments such as, $50.00 dollars per month that can be drawn against your bank account. Business people can put in a lump sum of, $500.00 dollars to open the account and can add to it as often as they like in what ever amount they want.

This allows the mutual fund to put thousands of people's money together and the mutual funds manager goes out and purchases stock in many major companies, therefore spreading your money around. Then again, some will gain and some others will lose, but if, you look at a 10-year performance, on a particular fund, you can see that generally they perform very well.

Personally, I would not invest in any mutual fund unless; it had at least, a 10-year track record of performance. When you look at a 10-year chart, you will see that in some years that particular fund will even lose money but, this is a long-term investment and very normal for that to happen. If, you get afraid and pull your money out, you will probably lose money.

In a one on one discussion with individuals, a licensed security agent is required by law to show you a perspective. In this perspective, it lists the names of companies and industries that, the mutual funds manager have invested people's money into. By law, if a licensed security agent mentions the name of a mutual fund, they must show you this perspective.

Many years ago, I became a licensed life, health and security agent and had discussed the securities (mutual funds) with my mother who had her money in a CD at a bank. After about 3 years of on and off discussion one day she asked me, "Well, just how safe are they?" I replied, "Mom, I assume, you are asking for the worst case scenario, which means, another depression." I went on to explain, that nearly 90% of all the banks in the country went under during the depression but, not one mutual fund company has ever went under, and I further explained when you get a guaranteed percentage rate then, you usually get a guaranteed loss.

By law, I also had to explain to people the benefits of a mutual fund for their age bracket. In my mother's case, a moderate risk, high growth mutual fund would not be the proper mutual fund to get her to invest her money into, but a lower yield; lower risk municipal bond would have been the proper one. However, she selected the higher growth fund after I showed her that, the average rate of return over the last 10 years for that particular fund was over 26%.

My mother attends church in a rural congregation that has an older crowd and when she told some of the ladies she was getting 26% where most of these women were getting less than 5% on a CD, you can imagine how difficult it was for them to believe her.

As I explained, this particular fund the next year might lose money however, as this turned out, in 6 months time the stocks split on this particular fund and my mother's money doubled. This, of course, would not happen very often.

In doing basic financial planning for middle class people during the period I was licensed, if, my memory serves me correctly, I showed a chart that showed the average individual setting aside $30.00 dollars a month over a 40 year period. I used this amount to show people that didn't think that $30.00 dollars a month would make a difference in their retirement. It indeed would if; it was put in the right place. Again, if memory serves me correctly (I will use approximate figures), the charts show setting aside thirty dollars a month in a CD that was drawing 4% and would yield the client thirty nine thousand dollars at retirement however, the same thirty dollars set aside in a good performing mutual fund that only produces 15% would yield the client about seven hundred thirty eight thousand dollars at retirement.

It certainly does make a lot of difference where you put your saving and its shows. If, you ever receive a statement from a credit card company, they're charging you 15%–23% and when you make a payment, the interest almost eats up all your payment. This is called Compound Interest.

Another good example is, I purchased a piece of residential property 5 years ago as I write this book, and I gave $99,900 for the property. A couple of years later, interest rates dropped dramatically so, I refinanced the house on a 20 year loan instead of a 30 year loan, my payments were increased by $13.00 more per month however, by getting a percent and a half lower interest rate and going from 30 years to 20 years, I saved over $100,000 in interest.

If, you decide that real estate is a field that, you would like to seek a new career in, you can do this on a part time basis without giving up your present job and risking the security that, you have to pay your present bills. In many cases, your approach will be that you are willing to give their price and their interest rate if, they're willing to give you your terms. But, as you can see, one or two per-cent points does make a lot of difference so, be careful about what you agree to do and my suggestion is, never give more than 10% interest on a owner carried note unless, you are positive you can make money on the deal. So, before you sign anything, do your homework.

The libraries and book stores are full of many books about real estate, written by several different authors, so, I suggest that, you read every one to get differ-ent ideas so, that you will know which field of real estate you want to work in, i.e., VA repossessions, FHA repossessions, foreclosed properties, etc.

I have one business acquaintance that used to teach at a small university but, retired when he was about 45 years old, because, for several years he had pur-chased property at public tax sales, fixed the property up with cosmetic things such as painting, carpet and wall paper and resold the houses, carrying the note himself at 10% interest with a minimum down payment. In other words he recovered the money that, he paid for the property through the tax sales. His new buyer's down payment covered this cost.

I have been asked many times about the programs that are available on tape from some of the T.V. gurus that, deal with no money down real estate and I have always affirmed that most of those have very good programs and can give you invaluable material and ideas in order for you to be successful in this field. On the next couple of pages, I have given you a compound interest table and it is very simple to use.

For example, lets say that you had two thousand dollars and you were getting 2% on your money at the end of 5 years, to find out where you would be you would multiply the two thousand dollars times the 5.3081 or in other words in each place where there is a comma after the first digit, just insert a decimal point on your calculator and you will find out how much money you will have. So, let say that you were getting 4% and you were putting in one thousand dol-lars per year at the end of 20 years you multiply the 30.9692 times one thousand dollars, but if, you go straight over and you are getting 8%, you would think, well I'm not that much better off by getting 8% rather than 4% but, you can see you will be nineteen thousand dollars better off. On the same 4% if, you were getting 12% you would have over 80 thousand dollars by putting in one thousand dollars per year so, again, it does make a difference where you put your money.

Simple vs. Compound Interest

The following two examples of methods of computing interest on a principal sum illustrate the differences between simple interest and compound interest. Both examples use a $100 principal and 7% interest.

Simple Interest

The interest rate is applied only to the original principal amount in computing the amount of interest.

Year	Principal ($)	Interest	Ending Balance
1	$100.00	7.00%	$107.00
2	$100.00	7.00%	$114.00
3	$100.00	7.00%	$121.00
4	$100.00	7.00%	$128.00
5	$100.00	7.00%	$135.00

Compound Interest

The interest rate is applied to the original principal and any accumulated interest.

Year	Principal ($)	Interest ($)	Ending Balance
1	$100.00	$7.00	$107.00
2	$107.00	$7.49	$114.49
3	$114.49	$8.01	$122.50
4	$122.50	$8.58	$131.08
5	$131.08	$9.18	$140.26

Compound interest has a larger effect as the time period increases and as the interest rate increases.

On the following pages are the compound interest tables.
These are calculated
at one dollar per annum.

End of Year	2%	2.50%	3%	3.50%	4%	4.50%	5%	5.50%
1	$1.0200	$1.0250	$1.0300	$1.0350	$1.0400	$1.0450	$1.0500	$1.0550
2	2.0604	2.0756	2.0909	2.1062	2.1216	2.1370	2.1525	2.1680
3	3.1216	3.1525	3.1836	3.2149	3.2465	3.2782	3.3101	3.3423
4	4.2040	4.2563	4.3091	4.3625	4.4163	4.4707	4.5256	4.5811
5	5.3081	5.3877	5.4684	5.5502	5.6330	5.7169	5.8019	5.8881
6	6.4343	6.5474	6.6625	6.7794	6.8983	7.0192	7.1420	7.2669
7	7.5830	7.7361	7.8923	8.0517	8.2142	8.3800	8.5491	8.7216
8	8.7546	8.9545	9.1591	9.3685	9.5828	9.8021	10.0266	10.2563
9	9.9497	10.2034	10.4639	10.7314	11.0061	11.2882	11.5779	11.8754
10	11.1687	11.4835	11.8078	12.1420	12.4864	12.8412	13.2068	13.5835
11	12.4121	12.7956	13.1920	13.6020	14.0258	14.4640	14.9171	15.3856
12	13.6803	14.1404	14.6178	15.1130	15.6268	16.1599	16.7130	17.2868
13	14.9739	15.5190	16.0863	16.6770	17.2919	17.9321	18.5986	19.2926
14	16.2934	16.9319	17.5989	18.2957	19.0236	19.7841	20.5786	21.4087
15	17.6393	18.3802	19.1569	19.9710	20.8245	21.7193	22.6575	23.6411
16	19.0121	19.8647	20.7616	21.7050	22.6975	23.7417	24.8404	25.9964
17	20.4123	21.3863	22.4144	23.4997	24.6454	25.8551	27.1324	28.4812
18	21.8406	22.9460	24.1169	25.3572	26.6712	28.0636	29.5390	31.1027
19	23.2974	24.5447	25.8704	27.2797	28.7781	30.3714	32.0660	33.8683
20	24.7833	26.1833	27.6765	29.2695	30.9692	32.7831	34.7193	36.7861
21	26.2990	27.8629	29.5368	31.3289	33.2480	35.3034	37.5052	39.8643
22	27.8450	29.5844	31.4529	33.4604	35.6179	37.9370	40.4305	43.1118
23	29.4219	31.3490	33.4265	35.6665	38.0826	40.6892	43.5020	46.5380
24	31.0303	33.1578	35.4593	37.9499	40.6459	43.5652	46.7271	50.1526
25	32.6709	35.0117	37.5530	40.3131	43.3117	46.5706	50.1135	53.9660
26	34.3443	36.9120	39.7096	42.7591	48.0842	49.7113	53.6691	57.9891
27	36.0512	38.8598	41.9309	45.2906	48.9676	52.9933	57.4026	62.2335
28	37.7922	40.8563	44.2189	47.9108	51.9663	56.4230	61.3227	66.7114
29	39.5681	42.9027	46.5754	50.6227	55.0849	60.0071	65.4388	71.4355
30	41.3794	45.0003	49.0027	53.4295	58.3283	63.7524	69.7608	76.4194
31	43.2270	47.1503	51.5028	56.3345	61.7015	67.6662	74.2988	81.6775
32	45.1116	49.3540	54.0778	59.3412	65.2095	71.7562	79.0638	87.2248
33	47.0338	51.6120	56.7302	62.4532	68.8579	76.0303	84.0670	93.0771
34	48.9945	53.9282	59.4621	65.6740	72.6522	80.4966	89.3203	99.2514
35	50.9944	56.3014	62.2759	69.0076	76.5983	85.1640	94.8363	105.7652
36	53.0343	58.7339	65.1742	72.4579	80.7022	90.0413	100.6281	112.6373
37	55.1149	61.2273	68.1594	76.0289	84.9703	95.1382	106.7095	119.8873
38	57.2372	63.7830	71.2342	79.7249	89.4091	100.4644	113.0950	127.5361
39	59.4020	66.4026	74.4013	85.5503	94.0255	106.0303	119.7998	135.6056
40	61.6100	69.0876	77.6633	87.5095	98.8265	111.8467	126.8398	144.1189
41	63.8622	71.8398	81.0232	91.6074	103.8196	117.9248	134.2318	153.1005
42	66.1595	74.6608	84.4839	95.8486	109.0124	124.2764	141.9933	162.5760

43	68.5027	77.5523	88.0484	100.2383	114.4129	130.9138	150.1430	172.5727
44	70.8927	80.5161	91.7199	104.7817	120.0294	137.8500	158.7002	183.1192
45	73.3306	83.5540	95.5015	109.4840	125.8706	145.0982	167.6852	194.2457
46	75.8172	86.6679	99.3965	114.3510	131.9454	152.6726	177.1194	205.9842
47	78.3535	89.8596	103.4084	119.3883	138.2632	160.5879	187.0254	218.3684
48	80.9406	93.1311	107.5406	124.6018	144.8337	168.8594	197.4267	231.4336
49	83.5794	96.4843	111.7969	129.9979	151.6671	177.5030	208.3480	245.2175

End of Year	6%	7%	8%	9%	10%	11%	12%	13%
1	$1.0600	$1.0700	$1.0800	$1.0900	$1.1000	$1.1100	$1.1200	$1.1300
2	2.1836	2.2149	2.2464	2.2781	2.3100	2.3421	2.3744	2.4070
3	3.3746	3.4399	3.5061	3.5731	3.6410	3.7097	3.7793	3.8498
4	4.6371	4.7507	4.8666	4.9847	5.1051	5.2278	5.3528	5.4803
5	5.9753	6.1533	6.3359	6.5233	6.7156	6.9129	7.1152	7.3227
6	7.3938	7.6540	7.9228	8.2004	8.4872	8.7833	9.0890	9.4047
7	8.8975	9.2598	9.6366	10.0285	10.4359	10.8594	11.2997	11.7573
8	10.4913	10.9780	11.4876	12.0210	12.5795	13.1640	13.7757	14.4157
9	12.1808	12.8164	13.4866	14.1929	14.9374	15.7220	16.5487	17.4197
10	13.9716	14.7836	15.6455	16.5603	17.5312	18.5614	19.6546	20.8143
11	15.8699	16.8885	17.9771	19.1407	20.3843	21.7132	23.1331	24.6502
12	17.8821	19.1406	20.4953	21.9534	23.5227	25.2116	27.0291	28.9847
13	20.0151	21.5505	23.2149	25.0192	26.9750	29.0949	31.3926	33.8827
14	22.2760	24.1290	26.1521	28.3609	30.7725	33.4054	36.2797	39.4175
15	24.6725	26.8881	29.3243	32.0034	34.9497	38.1899	41.7533	45.6717
16	27.2129	29.8402	32.7502	35.9737	39.5447	43.5008	47.8837	52.7391
17	29.9057	32.9990	36.4502	40.3013	44.5992	49.3959	54.7497	60.7251
18	32.7600	36.3790	40.4463	45.0185	50.1591	55.9395	62.4397	69.7494
19	35.7856	39.9955	44.7620	50.1601	56.2750	63.2028	71.0524	79.9468
20	38.9927	43.8652	49.4229	55.7645	63.0025	71.2651	80.6987	91.4699
21	42.3923	48.0057	54.4568	61.8733	70.4027	80.2143	91.5026	104.4910
22	45.9958	52.4361	59.8933	68.5319	78.5430	90.1479	103.6029	119.2048
23	49.8156	57.1767	65.7648	75.7898	87.4973	101.1742	117.1552	135.8315
24	53.8645	62.2490	72.1059	83.7009	97.3471	113.4133	132.3339	154.6196
25	58.1564	67.6765	78.9544	92.3240	108.1818	126.9988	149.3339	175.8501
26	62.7058	73.4838	86.3508	101.7231	120.0999	142.0786	168.3740	199.8406
27	67.5281	79.6977	94.3388	111.9682	133.2099	158.8173	189.6989	224.9999
28	72.6398	86.3465	102.9659	123.1354	147.6309	177.3972	213.5828	257.5834
29	78.0582	93.4608	112.2832	135.3075	163.4940	198.0209	240.3327	292.1992
30	83.8017	101.0730	122.3459	148.5752	180.9434	220.9132	270.2926	331.3151
31	89.8898	109.2182	133.2135	163.0370	200.1378	246.3236	303.8477	375.5161
32	96.3432	117.9334	144.9506	178.8003	221.2515	274.5292	341.4294	425.4632
33	103.1838	127.2588	157.6267	195.9823	244.4767	305.8374	383.5210	481.9034
34	110.4348	137.2369	171.3168	214.7108	270.0244	340.5896	430.6635	545.6808
35	118.1209	147.9135	186.1021	235.1247	298.1268	379.1644	483.4631	617.7493
36	126.2681	159.3374	202.0703	257.3759	329.0395	421.9825	542.5987	699.1867
37	134.9042	171.5610	219.3159	281.6298	363.0434	469.5106	608.8305	791.2110
38	144.0585	184.6403	237.9412	308.0665	400.4478	522.2667	683.0102	895.1984
39	153.7620	198.6351	258.0565	336.6824	441.5926	580.8261	766.0914	1012.7042
40	164.0477	213.6096	279.7810	368.2919	486.8518	645.8269	859.1424	1145.4858
41	174.9505	229.6322	303.2435	402.5281	536.6370	717.9779	963.3595	1295.5289
42	186.5076	246.7765	328.5830	439.8457	591.4007	798.0655	1080.0826	1465.0777

43	198.7580	265.1209	355.9496	480.5218	651.6408	886.9627	1210.8125	1656.6678
44	211.7435	284.7493	385.5056	524.8587	717.9048	985.6386	1357.2300	1873.1646
45	225.5081	305.7518	417.4261	573.1860	790.7953	1095.1688	1521.2176	2117.8060
46	240.0986	328.2244	451.9002	625.8628	870.9749	1216.7474	1704.8838	2394.2508
47	255.5645	352.2701	489.1322	683.2804	959.1723	1351.6996	1910.5898	2706.6334
48	271.9584	377.9990	529.3427	745.8656	1056.1896	1501.4965	2140.9806	3059.6258
49	287.3359	405.5289	572.7702	814.0836	1162.9085	1667.7712	2399.0182	3458.5071

<u>NOTES</u>

<u>NOTES</u>

<u>NOTES</u>

<u>NOTES</u>

Chapter 3

The Lease/Option

There are two parts to this. The lease which, is just like leasing a home. You have to make the agreed payments for the period of the lease. The seller cannot increase the rent nor raise the price. The second half is the option. You have an option to buy but, if, the value of the house does not increase as you have hoped for, you can simply walk away.

There is a lease/purchase agreement where you defiantly have to buy so, making sure of which, you are signing and this is why, you should always use your contract.

The whole idea is to lease a home with the option to purchase at a later date. You are wanting the value of the property to appreciate in value while, someone else lives in the home that you have subleased to, make the payments. You want to include a clause in the contract that allows you to sublease this house so:

Step 1:

You find a motivated seller. This is referred to in real estate terms as a "don't wanter". This means that, they do not want the house for some reason and it is usually because of a divorce, people being transferred, one of the two couples in a marriage have been laid off, etc. You can ask questions whenever you call about the property and find out why they are selling. If, you get a negative reaction to your questions and they want to know why you are asking you can say, "Well I mean, does your house sit on top of a grave or sink hole or anything like that". Most of the time, you will be surprised how liberal people are in giving you the information about why they are selling the house.

Step 2:

The property you are looking for should have been owned for at least 7 to 10 years. The reason for this is simple. You plan to sublease the house during the lease period so, you want lease payments that should not be above the going rental rates. If, you are confused on my statement, to clarify, if someone purchased a house recently then, their payments would be more than it would be as if, they purchased the house several years ago. The whole idea is to make enough payments to the person you are leasing from so that, they can cover their mortgage payments on this property.

Step 3:

At this point, you need to get a contract signed. Use your own, not a broker's. You need to include a weasel clause and tell the seller you will rent 30 days or less from the contract date. This allows you time to run a newspaper ad to find someone to sublet the house to. If, you don't, you can "weasel" out of the contract. You should include a clause that allows you to show the house if, it is still occupied. If, you do not know what a weasel clause is, it is wording in the contract that allows you to get out of the deal such as, "subject to my attorney's approval" or "subject to my partner's approval" or other terms that you can use that allows you to get out of the contract.

Step 4:

Run a newspaper ad to find your buyer. For example, let's say your price is $60,000.00 on this house. You add 2% or $1,200.00 to it and ask for the down payment of $1,200.00. The $1,200.00 is yours to put in your pocket now! You let the buyer you found pay the lease amount of say $500.00 per month but, you add $50.00 to that so, you pay the seller $500.00 and pocket $50.00 per month. So that, you are not confused about why you want to buy property that is 7 to 10 years old, one of the things that needs to be understood here is the reason. The homeowner is making payments to his mortgage company presently and should be less than the going rental rate so that you can add to that amount you agreed to pay on the lease. It can be $25.00, $50.00 or more depending, on the market going rate.

Step 5:

All the rent ($500.00 per month) your sublet renter pays is to go toward the purchase price so in this case, $6,000.00 per year. You have the seller to agree on a 5 year lease/option. You have a loan note at the end of the lease period so, at the end of five years, lets assume that the value of the house appreciated 5% per year, so at the end of the lease/option period, the house is now worth $76,757.00. This is what has happened by then:

1. $76,757.00—value after five years

2. $60,000.00—owed to the owner (your sublet gets this loan and you pay the seller).
$16,757.00—amount house appreciated (yours to keep). Your contract was sublet renters says they pay the appreciated value at the end of 5 years.

Here is the kicker. You pay the $500.00 per month toward the original price of $60,000.00 so, you only owe $30,000.00. You get $76,000.00, pay the owner $30,000.00 and you pocket $46,000.00. That not all. Besides the $1,200.00 down, you have $50.00 per month positive cash flow times 12 months equals $600.00 per year times 5 years equals $3,000.00 so, your total profit would be nearly $50,000.

What if, the seller will only agree to allow one half of the lease money that you are paying to them, to be applied against the selling price? You still win. Along with that, if, your selling price has to remain at $60,000.00, you would still get $1,200.00 down payment from your renter, one half applied to the purchase price would be $15,000.00 so you get $60,000.00, you pay the seller $45,000.00 and you still make $16,200.00 and clear about $15,000.00 with no money and no credit. Do one per month and you have $180,000.00 per year income? Not bad. Remember, your sublet renter, will be on a lease/purchase agreement, not a lease/option.

Always use a real estate attorney, none other, to draw up your own lease/option and lease/purchase agreements or other forms that, you will need in dealing in real estate. They are standard forms at most office supply places that, you may also use without having to go to the expense of an attorney.

All agreements should be notarized. The seller should sign a deed to the property and this should be put in a mutual dipositary (or escrow) with a clause saying it is to be delivered to you when you exercise the option. The events should be properly recorded at the county court house or, if you wish, a title company, for a small fee, will do it for you. This prevents a dishonest seller from selling the property out from under you or leasing it to someone else or taking out another mortgage on the property.

All payments should be made through a bank or escrow company and they make the payments to the seller.

Whoever buys from you on the contract must sign a quick claim deed and put it in escrow, to be delivered to you if, your renter is more than 30 days late on a payment. This is returned to your renter when he takes title by paying off the balloon note.

You need to include a heavy prepayment penalty of 10-20% of the purchase price on your buyer to discourage him from making an early payment and make sure the words, "or more" are not after the amount of the monthly payment. This would automatically give him the right to prepay and you do not want that.

You need to take out title insurance. This insures that the seller really does own the property and that; there are not hidden leans or mortgages against it.

As an added bonus to the seller and to help you negotiate the deal, you might like to know that any money that the seller receives on a lease /option is not taxable!

All transactions need to be recorded. You can control thousands of dollars in property for 4 to 7 years without any risk on your part and just sit back and let inflation do the job for you.

In keeping with the game plan of using little or none of your own money, what do you do if; a realtor is involved where the house is listed with her/him? They certainly will want their commissions. If, it sells or you agree to buy, even at a later day, they will expect the seller to pay the 6% fee that is generally charged and the seller, not getting any up front money from you, more than likely, would not want to fork out this money to the agent without getting at least that amount up front from you. Remember, you are a problem solver. Think. There is a simply solution if, you just use a little common sense.

First, remember a rule you always will need to use in real estate in order to achieve your goals. You get nothing in life unless you ask and the worst they can say is no. If, they say no, don't take it personally. You will get a bunch of no's. It only means that you will have to find another way to solve the problem. Think. What does the realtor want? His/her commission, right? Show them how they can get what they want by simply offering to pay their commission in monthly installments of say $25.00 per month. That is $300.00 a year and the balance to be due before or on the day your option expires. You then add this amount to the amount that you have your buyer pay you per month.

Granted, this may not be exactly the way that a realtor had in mind or had preferred to get his/her money but, it's better than losing a sale. If, the realtor is part time, you have an even a better chance because, they do not depend upon this money to pay their bills. So, now one problem is solved.

You just tell the seller that, you will pay the realtor's fee now if; he will take that as a down payment and apply it against the selling price.

There is a way to work every deal but, you must find a motivated seller and do that by qualifying them over the phone first.

You must learn how to negotiate and one of the main rules to remember is the first one to mention the price is the loser. They can no where but, down. Always ask for 100% of the lease monthly payments to be applied toward the purchase price and negotiate from there but, if you start at the middle (50%) you can only expect to go down and you cannot raise it up.

Once you have run a newspaper ad, the next thing you need to do is qualify the seller by asking the seller the following questions:

1. Name of seller/phone number (may I ask your name)

2. Tell me about your property (only ask questions about those items not listed in the ad)

A. How many bedrooms (looking for three bedroom homes)

B. How many baths (looking for 1 1/2 to 2 bath homes)

C. Does it have CHA (central heat and air)

D. Are there built in appliances

E. Is it carpet or hardwood

F. Brick or wood siding

G. What type of loan (looking for FHA/VA, assumable loans)

H. Are you payments current

I. Does payment include PIPI (principle, interest, taxes and insurance)

J. Do you mind if, I ask why you are selling

K. How long have you owned the property

L. How long has the property been on the market

M. Are there any renters in the neighborhood

N. Are you willing to assist in the financing

O. Would you consider leasing your property with an option to buy

When you get the answers to these questions then, you can decide if, this is a piece of property that you want to go look at and by qualifying the seller before you go, you will not waste near as much of your time.

Also, realize that once you find a motivated seller in the category that, you are looking for, you will probably only get about 1 out of every 20 that talk with you, however, remember how much money that one will make you.

Remember also, if, it was easy, every body would be doing it. This is not easy. It will take a lot of hard work and dedication just as any other job, in order to make this kind of money.

One thing to remember in negotiating real estate deals is that, there are as many deals available as, your mind can come up with. Think.

Let's look at another variation of a lease option and let's say in this case a realtor is involved and you will get only 25% of the lease payments applied to the purchase price. Let's assume also that the property definitely increases 5% per year. Your lease option is for five years so, you get the realtor to agree to take $25.00 per month toward their commission with the balance due on whenever, and you exercise your option. Let's say that, the house is a three bedroom, two baths which, is exactly what you are wanting and is located in a good neighborhood. This is another good thing to remember. You want the worst house in the best neighborhood whenever, you are purchasing real estate. Let's say that the seller has agreed to let the realtor's fee being paid by you, go toward the purchase price. The lease/option amount agreed on is $60,000. The seller has a mortgage payment of $500.00 per month. This is how the deal will be worked:

1. You do the negotiating. This may shock the realtor because realtors are not use to potential buyers going with them to present an offer but, trust me, you have every right in the world to be present. As I have previously said, use your contract and terms so that you can include the weasel clause. So, I have a house on contract with closing (lease) to become effective in 30 days. I have the right to show and sublease the house and that is why I want the 30 day period because, at the end of the 30 days if, I cannot find a subleaser, I can get out of the deal and not spend anything but, my time and gas.

2. You run a newspaper ad to find your buyer. You then have them pay you $550.00 per month for five years. You pay the seller $500.00, you pay realtor $25.00 and you keep $25.00 in your pocket every month in cash flow. 25% of your buyer's payment or $125.00 per month applies against the selling price. We find that at the end of the first year, at five percent appreciation, the house is worth $63,000.00 at the end of the first year, $66,150.00, at the end of the second year, $69,457.50, at the end of third year, $72,930.38 at the end of the fourth year and $76,576.90 at the end of the fifth year. Your buyer gets a new loan. Your selling price to them will be $75,500.00, less the $7,500.00 credit or $68,000.00. You get $68,000.00 dollars. You owe the seller $68,000.00 less, the realtor fee of $3,600.00 which, you get credit for and less the $7, .500.00 on the 25% of the rental applied against the selling price so, you owe a total of $48,900.00. You make $19,100.00 plus you cash flow $300.00 per year times five years or $1,500 plus, you got a down payment of anywhere from $500.00 up. You get a buyer on a lease/purchase agreement. If, the house loan is 90% of the market value, that would be $67,900.00 (90% of $75,500.00).

Let's say the house increases none in value. I pay the seller a closing $60,000.00 less $11,100.00 or $49,900.00. Your buyer gets a $54,000.00 loan (90% of $60,000.00). You still make $4,100.00 plus, the cash flow of $1,500.00 plus, the down payment. How many of these do you think you can do in a month's time especially, if, you were in a major city?

Always remember to use your thinking cap because, there are probably at least a thousand variations of this that, you can come up in order to work the deal on your behalf.

NOTES

<u>NOTES</u>

_____

_____

_____

_____

_____

_____

_____

_____

_____

_____

_____

_____

_____

_____

_____

NOTES

<u>NOTES</u>

_____

_____

_____

_____

_____

_____

_____

_____

_____

_____

_____

_____

_____

_____

_____

_____

Chapter 4

Double Close Technique

The purpose of this technique is, to enable an investor to borrow money as the owner instead of the buyer. Why? Because different rules apply. If, you are the buyer, all buyers must put up a cash down payment if, obtaining a loan through a mortgage company, no exceptions. Secondly, the maximum loan amount will be a percentage of the purchase price, assuming the purchase price is the appraised price or below. This is called a purchased money mortgage.

If, you are the owner, the type of loan you get is an equity loan (a loan against the equity in your property) as a second mortgage or, you refinance. There is no down payment, they will even loan you the closing cost and the loan amount will be based on the actual appraised value of the property instead of the sales price.

I want to emphasis as much as possible that, some of the techniques taught in this book may not be legal in your city or state and that is why, I have stressed that you need to work closely with a good real estate attorney.

The double close is a great way to purchase when you have a highly motivated seller who has a very large equity in the property and is willing to carry a second mortgage with part cash down or properties that have no mortgage.

Again, in the real estate contract that you use for this technique, be sure to add that, the contract is subject to a double closing-see attached addendum and attach a copy of the instructions to the escrow agent, which can be a title company or real estate attorney. An example of these closing instructions is included in the following pages. Also, be sure to enclose a "weasel clause" in the contract.

If, using a realtor includes a clause in the contract, "Buyer reserves the right to accompany listing agent when the offer is presented to the seller". Yes, I know this is unusual but, it is legal. The agent certainly will not like it but, you are within your rights and you need to be there to answer questions plus, make sure the agent doesn't undermine you and tell the seller that you are crazy. In fact, I would suggest that you accompany the realtor on any piece of property that you really want to purchase because, I have seen first hand how some realtors work and they do not carry the degree of integrity that they should in some cases. I have had many realtors tell me confidential information that the seller has given to them and should not have repeated but, in order to make the sale, they did.

Example Number 1: Double Closing
$60,000—Market Value (house will appraise for this)
-$30,000—Existing mortgage balance
$30,000—Sellers equity in the property

Bank will loan 80% of the market value or $48,000 on this property.

Seller wants $10,000 of the $30,000 equity at closing.

Seller will carry second mortgage for $20,000.

<u>How to Work the Deal</u>

1. Seller gives title on property to buyer before closing.

2. Buyer gives note to seller for $10,000 along with a quit claim deed. This protects the seller where he can get his property back in case the buyer doesn't close. The worst that would happen is, the seller would get their property back by using the quit claim deed.

3. The buyer is now the owner and obtains a new loan for 80% or $48,000.

A. The original loan of $30,000 balance is paid off

B. The $10,000 equity is paid to the seller

C. Closing costs are included in the loan because the buyer is the owner.

D. The escrow agent returns (destroys) the note of $10,000 along with the quit claim deed.

E. Buyer, after deducting minor costs, puts nearly $7,500 in his pocket, no money down.

F. The sellers' $20,000 second mortgage is now recorded. A note for the $20,000 being held by an escrow agent is now returned to the buyer.

Note: The escrow agent can be the realtor, real estate attorney or a title company.

Note: Ask the seller to put off getting his first payment for 25 months so, that you will have time to raise the rents to cover the second mortgage payments.

Note: If listed with a realtor, you can agree to pay the realtor in exchange for owing the second mortgage. This comes out of the money left over at closing.

As an added inducement for the seller to work the double close deal, you might use additional collateral such as putting up a second mortgage against your home, jewelry, automobile, etc. With the "weasel clause" contract, you have absolutely nothing to worry about.

Your deal with the seller should include a 90 day period after the property has been transferred to you. This gives you time to get a loan. It, of course, can be less than 90 days if, you get the loan ahead of time.

The whole purpose of the double close is to allow you to borrow money as the owner instead of the buyer.

If, impeded interest is a problem in closing, be willing to pay the tax liability. This means if, the seller is concerned about (or knows) the IRS will hit him for the tax liability, if he carries a second mortgage at an interest below what the IRS says they should charge. It is much better to pay a portion of an interest rate than to pay the full interest rate.

The double closing includes two basis types of normal closing:

A. Loan closing:
This is when a loan is approved when the note is signed

B. Transaction closing:

This is when no loan is being obtained but, real estate is changing hands, such as your parents give you a house.

In the double closing, the property is transferred to the buyer which, is now the owner and the "buyer" obtains a new loan. The note is signed, the mortgage, liens, realtor and Etc. is all paid off and monies left over, belong to the buyer.

The buyer now has a transaction with the seller, at a later date, that gives the seller the cash agreed on and the escrow agent will record the second mortgage being carried by the seller. This is a transaction closing.

Equitable title can be transferred to the "buyer" by the use of a deed, real estate contract or a land contract .

Legal title is held only when a person owns a property free and clear. In any event, Equitable title should be recorded no matter what means is used so that, the bank will find That you own the property when, they do a title search.

Example of escrow agent instructions Number 1

To the escrow agent:

Please proceed with the following instructions in the order given. All changes to the following must be in writing, dated and approved by all of the parties to the transaction.

Pre-Closing Instructions

1. Review purchase agreement.

2. Escrow the ernest money.

3. Prepare warranty deed from seller to buyer on subject property.

4. Prepare warranty deed from buyer to seller on the collateral property.

5. Prepare quit claim deeds on both properties to return properties to their respective owners in the event that, financing is unavailable.

First Closing Instructions

6. Seller to execute a warranty deed for the subject property in favor of the buyer.

7. Buyer to execute a quit claim deed on the subject property.

8. Buyer to execute a warranty deed on his own home to be used as collateral in favor of the seller.

9. Seller to execute a quit claim deed on the collateral property.

10. Escrow agent shall record both warranty deeds and hold both quit claim deeds in escrow for a period not to exceed 90 days without further written instructions, signed by both parties. If, the rest of these instructions are not completed to the satisfaction of both parties within 90 days then, the escrow agent shall release and record the quit claim deeds. Both parties shall then receive their respective properties back. Under these circumstances any ernest money shall be returned to the buyer.

11. Buyer shall proceed to make necessary repairs on the subject property sufficient to get the property rented and refinanced.

12. When the refinance is completed, the full purchase price $_____ shall be dispersed to the seller. The escrow agent shall assist the bank in distributing the proceeds of a new loan.

13. The escrow agent shall release and record the quit claim deed on the collateral property.

14. The escrow agent shall destroy the quit claim deed on the subject property.

Seller _____ Date _____

Buyer _____ Date _____

Example of escrow agent instructions Number 2

To the escrow officer:

Please proceed with the following instructions in the order given.

Any changes to the following must be in writing and signed by all parties to the transaction. These instructions are an addendum to the purchase agreement dated _____, referring to the purchase of real estate property located at <u>Address, City and State</u> between the Seller _____ and the Buyer _____ shall be a legal and binding part of the purchase agreement.

1. Escrow agent shall prepare a real estate contract for the parties to transfer equitable ownership of the subject property from the seller to the buyer with a contract price of $_____ and the balance of the contract due and payable 90 days after it is executed.

2. Escrow agent shall prepare a quit claim deed from the buyer back to the seller on the subject property to be recorded only in the event the buyer fails to perform under said agreement by obtaining financing necessary to cash out the seller.

3. Both the above mentioned documents, contract and quit claim deed shall be executed by the respective parties.

4. The escrow officer shall release and record the real estate contract (notice of contract) but, shall hold the quit claim deed by the buyer refinances his subject property, the quit claim deed shall be held for a period not to exceed 60 days.

<u>NOTES</u>

<u>NOTES</u>

_____

_____

_____

_____

_____

_____

_____

_____

_____

_____

_____

_____

_____

_____

_____

_____

NOTES

<u>NOTES</u>

_____

_____

_____

_____

_____

_____

_____

_____

_____

_____

_____

_____

_____

_____

_____

_____

Chapter 5

Equity Sharing Technique

This concept can be used in many different ways, either by self or in conjunction with other creative financing tools.

Example

<u>How it works:</u>

1. You find a motivated seller (a don't wanter)

A. A couple getting a divorce.

B. A seller being transferred.

C. A seller living out of state or out of town.

D. A seller that is laid off work or behind on their payment for any reason.

E. A house that is vacant for any reason.

F. A seller wanting to build or buy another home.

2. Negotiate terms, sign contract (yours), tie up house for as long as possible (30 to 90 days) using a legal clause. (This allows time to find another buyer.)

A. Subject to satisfactory life inspection

B. Subject to the advice of counsel

C. Subject to partner's approval

D. Subject to satisfactory financing

Note: The weasel clause allows you to back out at any time and the above wording is some that you can use in order to use the weasel clause.

3. Run a newspaper ad—find some else to make payments

4. Seller refinances his house on an assumable loan.

A. Seller gets most of his equity out

B. Buyer assumes loan (new loan)

C. Seller carries a second mortgage on the balance

D. Instead of an interest rate on the second mortgage, seller gets a percent of ownership in the property (lets say 10% for an example)

E. Buyer finds another "buyer" and gets 50% ownership

F. By retaining 40% ownership, seller retains 10% ownership and you "buyer" get 50% ownership.

The benefits for all four of these are shown on the following pages with an example on how this technique may work.

Equity Sharing Example

$80,000—appraised price
$60,000—loan balance
$20,000—owner's equity

1.Owner wants fair market value—gets it.

2.Owner wants $10,000 cash equity, carries a second mortgage on the balance.

Creative Financing:

A. Owner refinances home, gets 90% loan ($72,000)

B. Closing costs are added to second mortgage.

C. Buyer assumes $72,000 first mortgage (cost to buyer—approximately $45.00)

D. Owner receives $12,000 after old loan of $60,000 is paid off.

E. Seller receives 10% ownership instead of 10% interest on second mortgage

Seller Benefits:

1. Gets 12% appreciation value on total amount of the house.

2. Get 12% depreciation on full value per year tax ride off.

3. Get 12% of the amount paid on the principle.

4. No realtor fees

5. Avoids possible lost of rent, vandalism, credit problems and etc.

Buyer Benefits:

1. Little or no money down.

2. Tax ride off on depreciation

3. Owns instead of rents—gets appreciation value.

4. No credit needed.

The typical offer would be:

A. Buyer assumes present loan

B. Buyer pays $10,000 cash down (this is the problem that you solve)

C. Seller carries a second mortgage

An offer is made to a potential seller using this technique or any other techniques except for the lease option, you will need to sit down with your offer and draw out similar to what I have here so that the seller will be able to understand what you are talking about. I learned a lesson many years ago that for instance, in religion, you are totaling wasting your time discussing religion with another person if you differ in opinion unless you have an open bible and can show them. The same rule applies in trying to purchase real estate with little or no money down using creative financing techniques.

Especially since I would never bend my morals and doing anything illegal or immoral to get ahead in business, many people ask me how in the world that I made it in business. I usually reply that I wanted to success almost to the point of being fanatical and that I just worked my fanny off and gave up many of the pleasures that people go out and enjoy in order to be able to do that every day at an early age and not retire when I have one foot in the grave.

If, I included every possible way that you can purchase real estate with little or no money down, I would probably have a 700 to 1,000 page book so, my book is not by any means a "bible" on no money down real estate but, I hope that I have accomplished getting your mind to start thinking in a total different direction of the opportunities that are out here in America and this field is one of many.

If, I accomplish that then I will certainly feel good that I have taken the time to write this book whether I make any money on it or not because, that was not my purpose and if I do make any money, 50% of it after deducting all my costs will be given to different charities and especially the batter and abused centers. Please do not let your mind stop with just the technique that I have shown you because there are probably a thousand variations of those that I have already shown you and whatever your mind can come up with that would be agreeable with you and the seller will work.

In order to be successful in this business or any other business I feel you need to follow the following:

A. Never pay the asking price unless (double close)

B. Keep your case outlayed to a bare minimum

C. Become a wheeler dealer

D. Use other peoples money for as much and as long as possible

E. Work business deals fast or in other words don't scratch your rear-end make up your mind.

F. Develop unusual creative financial plans

G. Stay as deep in debt as possible with comfort

H. Have the courage to act

I. Try many different alternative routes

J. You must have a strong desire to become wealthy

K. You must see (a picture) enjoying the good life

L. You must seek opportunities to meet your goals

M. You must be willing to pay the price of being successful

<u>NOTES</u>

NOTES

<u>NOTES</u>

_____

_____

_____

_____

_____

_____

_____

_____

_____

_____

_____

_____

_____

_____

_____

_____

NOTES

Chapter 6

Real Estate Definitions

Acceleration Clause: A clause in a mortgage that gives the lender the right to demand payment of the principle balance if, a regular monthly payment is missed.

Acceptance: A person's consent to enter into a contract and be bound by the terms of the offer that he/she has made.

Additional Principle Payment: An additional payment by a borrower that exceeds the scheduled principle amount due in order to reduce the remaining balance on the loan.

Adjustable Rates: This is an interest rate that will increase or decrease according to the market.

Adjustable Rate Mortgage (ARM): A mortgage that allows the lender to adjust the interest rate on a loan on the basis of changes in a specified index.

Adjusted Basis: The original cost of the property plus any capital expenditures for improvement to the property minus any depreciation.

Adjustment period: The time that elapses between the adjustment dates for an adjustable rate mortgage. (ARM)

Adjustment Rate: The rate on which the interest rate may change for an adjustable rate mortgage. (ARM)

Administrator: A person appointed by a probate court to administer the state of a person who passed away.

Affordability Analysis: A detailed analysis of a person's ability to afford the purchase of a home. This analysis takes into consideration your income, available monies, liabilities, and assets on other assets, along with the type of mortgage that you plan to purchase. The closing cost that you may have on this loan and where the property is located is also considered.

Alternative Financing: Mortgage options available below market rate including ARM's, buy down's and graduated payment mortgages (GPM's).

Amenity: This is something about the property that gives more attractiveness and makes the property more desirable although that particular feature is not as necessary for the properties used. These can include a desirable location, a swimming pool, tennis court, community buildings, and other amenities such as being close to water or recreational facilities.

Amortization: The gradual repayment of a mortgage loan by making installments.

Amortization Schedule: The amortization schedule shows the amount of each payment and how much is applied to interest and how much is applied to principle, and then shows the remaining balance as each payment is made.

Amortization term: This is the required time to amortize the loan as shown in a number of months. As an example, a 20-year fixed rate mortgage would have an amortization term of 240 months.

Amortize: When a mortgage is paid with regular payments they cover both principle and interest.

Annual Mortgagor Statement: This is a report sent to the buyer at the end of each year. This report shows how much was paid in and how much was applied to principle and how much was applied to interest and also shows the remaining balance along with how much was paid for city and county taxes along with home owners insurance.

Annual Percentage Rage (APR): The percentage rate that you would have to pay on an annual basis for a mortgage, loans, or credit cards.

Annuity: The amount paid on a regular or yearly basis and is often paid on a guaranteed dollar basis.

Application: A form that records information about an individual or individual when applying for a mortgage loan.

Appraisal: A written estimate of the value of a piece of property that is prepared by licensed appraiser.

Appraised Value: The written opinion of a qualified appraiser as to the fair market value of a piece of property which is based on the appraiser's experience and knowledge of the market.

Appraiser: A licensed individual that is qualified to estimate the value of real and personal property based on his training and experience.

Appreciation: The increase in the value of a piece of property due to changes in market conditions or other factors.

Assessed Value: The value placed on a piece of property by an elected public tax assessor for purposes of taxation.

Assessment: The process that a tax appraiser uses in placing the value on a piece of property for the sole purpose of taxation.

Assessment Rolls: The public record of taxable property.

Assessor: An elected public official who places the value on a piece of property for taxation purposes.

Asset: Any property of monetary value that is owned by a person. These items would include real property, personal property, and judgment claims against others.

Assignment: The transfer of a mortgage from one person to another.

Assumable Loan: Usually for a small assumption fee, a new buyer can take over or assume the loan of the previous homeowner, saving closing costs and loan origination fees. Some are non-qualifying most are through qualification.

Assumable Mortgage: A mortgage that can be transferred from the seller to the buyer when a home is sold.

Assumption: This is the same thing as assumable mortgage or in other words, it's when an existing mortgage is transferred from the seller to the buyer.

Assumption Clause: A clause in the seller's mortgage that allows the buyer to assume responsibility of the existing mortgage. This clause allows the property to be transferred without the mortgage being paid in full by the seller.

Assumption Fee: An amount paid to the mortgagee that was a result of the transfer of an existing mortgage from the seller to the buyer.

Attorney–In–Fact: A person who holds a power of attorney from another to execute documents on behalf of that person.

Balance Sheet: A person's financial statement that would show his/her assets, liabilities, and net worth as of a certain date.

Balloon Mortgage: A mortgage that has even monthly payments that will amortize over a certain period of time and provides for a lump-sum payment to be due at the end of an earlier set time.

Balloon Payment: The lump-sum payment that is made at the maturity date of a balloon mortgage.

Bankrupt: An individual, company, or corporation that is relieved from the payment of debts to their creditors. They must first give up all of their assets to a court-appointed trustee.

Bankruptcy: A federal court proceeding in which the debtor is relieved of legal responsibility in payment of debts owed and who owes more than he or she has in assets. Chapter seven bankruptcies will relieve that person completely. However, there are other repayment plans where income is distributed by the courts and the bankruptcy notice to the creditors keeps the creditors from proceeding with any legal action against the debtor.

Before Tax Income: This is income before federal and/or state income taxes are deducted.

Beneficiary: A person designated by another party to receive income from a trust, estate, or a deed of trust.

Bequeath: Personal property that has been willed to another person.

Betterment: Repairs or additions to a piece of property that increases the property value.

Bill of Sale: A written document that transfers ownership title on personal property.

Binder: This is when a buyer offers to purchase real estate and secures the agreement by putting down a certain amount of earnest money deposit.

Biweekly Mortgage Payment: A mortgage payment that is made every two weeks instead of the standard monthly schedule. This reduces the debt and saves interest money because the payment is made every two weeks instead of on a monthly basis.

Blanket Insurance Policy: A policy that covers more than one person or piece of property.

Blanket Mortgage: A mortgage that is secured by a cooperative project such as a condominium community.

Bona Fide: When a person is acting in good faith and without fraud or deceit.

Bond: A debt of a government or business that has an interest-bearing certificate along with a maturity date. A real estate bond is normally secured by a mortgage or a deed of trust.

Breach: When a person violates a legal obligation or agreement.

Bridge Loan: A form of a second trust that is secured by the borrower's present home in a way that allows the proceeds to be used for closing on a new home even before the present home is sold.

Broker (Mortgage): An individual or company that for a fee acts as an intermediary between borrowers and lenders.

Broker (Real Estate): A person who receives a commission or other type of fee for assisting and negotiating contracts between two parties and is usually a real estate broker or a mortgage broker.

Budget: A written guideline of expected income in expenses over a given period of time and is used for managing future investments and expenses.

Budget Category: A category of income and expense information that can be used in a budget.

Building Code: Local, state, and/or federal regulations that control the construction of property and the materials used therein and is also based on safety and health standards.

Buydown Account: This is usually a mortgage account where funds are held in escrow so that payment on a mortgage can be applied as part of the monthly payment as each payment comes due during a certain period that an interest rate buydown plan is in effect.

Buydown Mortgage: A temporary buydown is a mortgage in which an initial lump-sum payment can be made to partly reduce the borrower's monthly payments during the first few years of a mortgage and a permanent buydown reduces interest rate over the entire life of that mortgage.

Call Option: A clause in a mortgage that gives the mortgagee the right to call or in other words foreclose on the mortgage and is payable at the end of a set period of time for any reason.

Cap: A clause in an adjustable rate mortgage that puts a limit on how much the interest and/or mortgage payments can be increased.

Capital: The total wealth of a business or person which, can also be the net worth of a business whereby assets exceeds their liabilities. It can also be a combination of money or property that totals the wealth owned by personal business enterprise.

Capital Expenditure: The cost of improvements that is used to extend the life of a piece of property or add to its value.

Capital Improvement: Any addition to a permanent piece of property that is used to improve that property or to increase its value or to extend the usefulness of that property.

Cash Flow: A term that real estate investors use whereby the amount of money that is available each month after paying out all debts.

Cash Out: This is usually where a second mortgage is put on a home in order for the home owner to receive the equity through a home equity loan.

Cash Out Refinance: This is similar to cash out except this is where the home owner refinances the existing mortgage and receives cash at closing that can be used for any purpose.

Cash Reserve: A requirement of some lenders that buyers have sufficient cash remaining after closing to make for first two monthly mortgage payments.

Certificate of Deposit: A written instrument issued by the bank or other financial institution that promises to return the amount deposited plus interest earnings at a set interest rate within a set period of time.

Certificate of Deposit Index: An index on certain ARM plans that is used to determine interest rate changes and represents the weekly average of market interest rates on six-month negotiated certificates of deposits.

Certificate of Eligibility: This is a document obtained from the Department of Veterans' Affairs for VA mortgages that certifies a veteran's eligibility.

Certificate of Reasonable Value: Another document issued by the VA that establishes the maximum value of the property and loan amount on a VA mortgage.

Certificate of Title: A statement that the title to a certain piece of real estate is legally held by the current owner and is usually obtained from an attorney, title company, or abstract company.

Chain of Title: A history of all the transfers made on a parcel of real estate property and starts with the earliest existing document and stops with the most recent.

Change Frequency: This refers to the payment in months and/or interest rate changes to an adjustable rate mortgage.

Chattel: This is another name that is used for personal property.

Clear Marketable Title: A title that is free of liens or legal questions as to the ownership of property.

Closed—End Home Equity Loan: A loan that is for a set period of time.

Closed In-Home Equity Loan: This is a loan that is for a specific term.

Closing: This is usually a meeting where a sale of a piece of property is completed by the buyer in signing the mortgage documents and paying any closing costs or in which the seller pays the closing costs.

Closing Costs: This is expenses that are involved in purchasing or refinancing a home such as: termite inspections and other fees connected with preparing the paperwork for closing.

Closing Cost Item: These are individual items that have to be paid at closing for a service items such as: termite inspection, attorney fees and other costs that are made up of costing cost items.

Cloud On Title: When a title search is done and items are found that would not allow a clear title to be given to a piece of property such as: IRS leans or other leans.

Co-Insurance: Many policies require the insured to carry a certain percentage of coverage based on the market value of a piece of property. When this coverage is not properly carried, the insurance company will depreciate any loss.

Co-Insurance Clause: There is a provision in the policy that a certain percentage of the market value of the property has to be carried as coverage otherwise; the property would be subject to depreciate in case of a loss.

Collateral: This is where a person has equity in a piece of property and they put that up as security for additional loan.

Collections: This is a process that is used in an attempt to bring a mortgage current when the homeowner is behind on payments and includes the process of foreclosure when it becomes necessary.

Co-Maker: This is a person who signs a loan agreement along with the original borrower and guarantees that if the borrower does not make the payment they will.

Combined LTV: LTV means the loan to value and a lender calculates the LTV on a home equity loan and it is a combination of the sum of the debts on both mortgages compared to the fare market value of a home.

Commission: This is the percentage of the sale price of a piece of property that is usually charged by a real estate broker or agent for negotiating the real estate transaction.

Commitment letter: The conditions that a lender makes in writing under which the lender agrees to loan money to a buyer.

Community Home Buyer's Program: An alternative financing option that allows households to modest means to qualify for mortgages using nontraditional credit histories, 33 percent housing-to-income and 38 percent debt-to-income ratios, and the waiver of the usual two payments cash reserves at closing.

Community Property: In some states, this is a form of ownership when property is acquired during the marriage and is assumed to be owned jointly, unless the property is acquired separately by either spouse.

Compound Interest: Interest paid on the original principle balance and the unpaid interest.

Condemnation: The determination, usually by a building code inspector, that a piece of property is not fit for human occupancy and/or is dangerous and must be destroyed. It can also be the taking of private property under the right of eminent domain for public use.

Condominium: A form of property ownership in which the homeowner holds title to an individual dwelling unity plus an interest in common areas of a multi-unit project, and sometimes the exclusive use of certain limited common areas.

Conforming Loan: Would be one that would follow very strict guidelines for eligibility a non-conforming loan has a wide range of programs that can be suited to fit individual circumstances.

Construction Loan: A short term loan, that lenders make to builders where they give the builder a progressive construction draw as the work progresses.

Consumer Reporting Agency: A firm that keeps track of borrower's credit history and reports this to lenders upon request.

Contingency: A condition that must be met before a contract is legally binding.

Contract: An agreement that can be either written or oral to do or not to do a specific thing.

Conventional Mortgage: Any mortgage that is not insured or guaranteed by the federal government.

Convertible ARM: An adjustable-rate-mortgage that can be converted to a fixed-rate mortgage under specified conditions.

Cooperative: A type of multiple ownership in which the residents of a multi-unit housing complex own shares in the corporation that owns the property, giving each resident the right to occupy a specific apartment or unit.

Covenant: A clause in a mortgage that obligates or restricts the borrower and that, if violated, can result in foreclosure.

Conventional Mortgage: A mortgage that is generally made by a bank but not insured or guaranteed by the federal government.

Convertible ARM: An adjustable rate mortgage that can be changed to a fixed rate mortgage under certain conditions.

Covenant: A clause in a mortgage that obligates or restricts the borrower and that, if violated, can result in foreclosure.

Credit: This is when a person borrows money or receives property in exchange for the promise to repay at a later time.

Credit History: This is a record of a person's past history of how they have handled their debts that allows a potential lender to determine whether that person has a good repayment history or not.

Credit Life Insurance: This is a type of life insurance that many lenders try to get people to take out as, it will pay off a mortgage, car loan, etc. in the event that the policyholder dies before the debt is paid off. I might add that, mortgage insurance is the same thing as life insurance and life insurance is sold by the thousand or, in other words, the older you get the more it will cost you per thousand. Never take out this type of coverage because, the cost per thousand is generally much more than what it would be if, you went out on the market and purchased a good cheap term insurance policy.

Credit Rating: This rating is based on your record of payment of your bills and determines your eligibility for any future loans.

Credit Report: These are prepared by a credit bureau and contain the credit history of an individual as to whether this person has a good history of repayment of debts in a timely manner.

Credit Worthiness: A lender will determine whether a loan is to be made to you based on your history that contains information as to your repayment history and ability.

Creditor: A person or company that you have borrowed money from.

Debt: This is an amount that is owed to another individual or company that you have borrowed on an installment loan.

Debt Consolidation: This is when an additional loan is obtained in order to pay off other loans that may have a high interest rate.

Debt—Reduction Plan: This is a plan to make varies moves such as consolidating debt in order to pay off higher interest credit cards or other debt to reduce the amount of debt owed.

Debt Service: This is the combined interest and principle that you pay on your loans and other debts.

Debt—To—Income Ratio: This is the amount of your monthly income that is used to pay off all of your debt obligations.

Deed: This is a legal instrument that gives title to you on a piece of property.

Deed of Trust: Some states use this document instead of a mortgage and the title is put into a trust.

Default: This is when a person fails to make payments as agreed on a debt.

Delinquency: This is when a person fails to make payments on a debt when they are due.

Depreciation: This is when a piece of property declines in value and can be due to such circumstances as failure to keep the property in good repair, a landfill being put nearby or other things that adversely affect the value of the property.

Disclosure: Document which describes all conditions of mortgage loan including terms and interest rates.

Discount Points: A one-time charge by the lender to increase the yield of the loan. A point is one percent of the amount of the mortgage.

Dower: This is the right that a widow has to the property of her husband when he dies.

Down Payment: This is upfront money that is paid by the buyer and is part of the purchase price however, it is not financed with the mortgage.

Due-On-Sale Provision: A clause in a mortgage that gives the lender the right to demand repayment on the total loan if, the buyer sells the property.

Earnest Money: An amount agreed on between the real estate agent and the buyer to show that he/he is serious about purchasing the piece of property and is refundable to the buyer upon purchasing the property.

Easement: This is access granted to a person or persons other than the owner to a piece of property.

Eminent Domain: This is right of the government to take private party for public use. This includes payment to the property owner of fair market value of the property.

Encroachment: This is when an improvement on a persons property that illegally intrudes on another persons property.

Encumbrance: This is anything that affects the title to a piece of property and includes but not limited mortgages, leins, easements or restrictions.

Endorser: The signature of a person that gives ownership over to another person or persons.

Equal Credit Opportunity Act: A federal law that requires lenders and other creditors to make credit equally available to borrowers without discrimination based on race, color, religion, national origin, age, sex, martial status or receipt of any income from public assistance programs.

Equity: This is the difference between the market value of a piece of property and the amount that is still owed on the mortgage.

Equity loan: A loan based on the borrower's equity on her or her home.

Escrow: Something of value that is deposited with a third party and is to be given to another party upon fulfillment of a condition or contract.

Escrow Account: The account of which something of value is held by a third party and is generally used for paying expenses that are against a piece of property, i.e., homeowners insurance, taxes, etc.

Escrow Payment: This is a part of a buyer's monthly payment that goes into a separate account for payment of property insurance, land taxes and other items that become due against the property.

Estate: This is the total amount of real and personal properties value at the time an individual dies.

Eviction: This is when a person is removed from a piece of property, usually rental property and is done so with the proper legal documents.

Executor: A person or persons named in another person's will to administrate an estate.

Exclusive Agency Listing: A listing contract in which the agent has the sole right to sell the home, though the sellers are not bound to pay the commission if they produce the buyer.

Exclusive Right-To-Sell Contract: A listing contract in which the seller gives the real estate broker the sole right to sell; the person receives a commission, regardless of who produces the buyer.

Earned Income: This is income from commissions, salary or business profits.

Fair Credit Reporting Act: A consumer protection law that regulates the disclosure of consumer/credit reports by consumer/credit agencies and establishes procedures for correcting mistakes on one's credit record.

Fair Market Value: This is what your house should sell for as compared to other properties similar to yours.

FHA Mortgage: A mortgage that is insured by the Federal Housing Administration. Also referred to as a "government" mortgage.

First Mortgage: The document that allows the mortgage holder to secure your loan if, you fail to me your obligations as an agreed.

First Lien: This gives the lender the right to foreclose on your property if, you fail to make the payments as agreed.

Fixed Rates: A fixed rate of interest that stays the same over the term of the loan.

Flood Insurance: Insurance that compensates for physical property damages resulting from flooding. It is required for properties located in federally designated flood areas.

Forbearance: The lender's postponement of foreclosure to give the borrower time to catch up on overdue payments.

Graduated Payment Mortgage (GPM): A mortgage that starts with low monthly payments that increase at the predetermined rate. The initial monthly payments are set at an amount lower than that required for full amortization of the debt.

Hazard Insurance: Insurance coverage that compensates for physical damage to a property from fire, wind, vandalism, or other hazards.

Home Equity: This is the money difference between what you owe on a piece of property and its actual market value.

Home Equity Line of Credit: This is when you borrow money against the equity in your home.

Homeowner's Insurance: An insurance policy that combines personal liability coverage and hazard insurance coverage for a dwelling and its contents.

Homeowner's Warranty (HOW): A type of insurance that covers repairs to specified parts of the house for a specified period of time. It is provided by the builder or property seller as a condition of the sale.

Impound: The portion of a borrower's monthly payments held by the lender to pay taxes, hazard insurance, and mortgage insurance.

Index: The interest rate to which changes in an adjustable-rate-mortgage are pegged.

Index Rate: The lenders usually charge a certain amount above what the index rate is and the index rate is determined according to the general market rates.

Interest: A rate at which a lender agrees to finance a loan.

Late Charge: The penalty a borrower must pay when a payment is made after the due date.

Lien: A legal claim against a property that must be paid off when the property is sold.

Lifetime Cap: A provision of an ARM that limits the highest rate that can occur over the life of the loan.

Listing Contract: A contract with a broker or firm the sellers hire to represent them in the sale of their home, according to the terms of sale that they specify. In exchange for producing a ready-willing-and-able buyer, the agent is paid a commission.

Loan Application: A form that is normally used and provided by a lender to take information as to the credit worthiness of a borrower.

Loan Application Fee: A lender's fee, usually ranging from $75 to $300, which the buyer must pay when applying for a mortgage.

Loan Commitment: A formal offer by a lender stating the terms under which it agrees to lend money to a home buyer.

Loan Origination Fee: A fee charged by the lender for processing a mortgage.

Loan Proceeds: The amount of money that you receive when your loan is approved.

Loan Servicing: The collection of mortgage payments from borrowers and related responsibilities of a loan servicer.

Loan-to-Value Ratio (LTV): The relationship between the unpaid principal balance of the mortgage and the appraised value (or sales price if it is lower) of the property.

Lock-In: A written agreement guaranteeing the home buyer a specified interest rate provided the loan is closed within a set period of time. The lock-in also usually specifies the number of points to be paid at closing.

Margin: The set percentage the lender adds to the index rate to determine the current interest rate of an ARM.

Market Rate: The average rate charged by lenders for conventional, fixed-rate loans.

Mortgage Banker: A company that originates mortgages exclusively for resale in the secondary market.

Mortgage Broker: An individual or company that for a fee acts as an intermediary between borrowers and lenders.

Mortgage Insurance: (Also known as Private Mortgage Insurance (PMI)) Insurance provided by nongovernmental insurers that protect lenders against loss if a borrower defaults. Fannie Mae generally requires private mortgage insurance for loans with loan-to-value (LTV) ratios greater than 80 percent.

Mortgage Insurance Premium (MIP): The fee paid by a borrower to FHA or a private insurer for mortgage insurance.

Mortgage Note: A legal document obligating a borrower to repay a loan at a stated interest rate during a specified period of time; the mortgage note is secured by a mortgage.

Mortgagee: The lender in a mortgage agreement.

Mortgagor: The borrower in a mortgage agreement.

Multiple Listing Service (MLS): A networking system, frequently on computer, in which a number of real estate firms share information about their client's homes that are for sale.

Negative Amortization: A gradual increase in the mortgage debt that occurs when the monthly payment is not large enough to cover the entire principal and interest due. The amount of the shortfall is added to the unpaid principal balance to create "negative" amortization.

Notice of Default: A formal written notice to a borrower that a default has occurred and that legal action may be taken.

Offer to Purchase and Acceptance: An offer of purchase that has been signed by both buyer and seller. A firm contract that outlines all details of the property transaction. Also known as a contract of sale or sales contract.

Offer to Purchase or Purchase Offer: A document that list the price, conditions, and terms under which the buyer is willing to purchase a property. Also known as an earnest money agreement, contract of purchase or deposit receipt.

Open Listing: A listing contract in which sellers hire more than one firm or person to sell their home, and only the one who produces the buyer is entitled to the commission.

Origination Fee: A fee paid to a lender for processing a loan application; it is stated as a percentage of the mortgage amount.

Payment Cap: A provision of some ARM's limiting the amount by which a borrower's payments may increase regardless of any interest rate increase; may result in amortization.

PITI: Acronym for principal, interest, taxes, and insurance—the components of a monthly mortgage payment.

Points: A one time charge by the lender to increase the yield of the loan; a point is 1 percent of the amount of the mortgage.

Pre-Approval: The process of determining that a borrower is credit approved up to a predetermined amount. The borrower is credit approved pending the locating of the home that meets the predetermined loan criteria.

Prepayment Penalty: A fee that may be charged to a borrower who pays off a loan before it is due.

Prequalification: The process of determining how much money a prospective home buyer will be eligible to borrow before a loan is applied for.

Principal: The amount borrowed or remaining unpaid; also, that part of the monthly payment tat reduces the outstanding balance of a mortgage.

Private Mortgage Insurance (PMI): Insurance provided by nongovernmental insurers that protect lenders against loss if a borrower defaults. Fannie Mae generally requires private mortgage insurance for loans with a loan-to-value (LTV) percentage greater than 80 percent.

Purchase and Sale Agreement: A written contract signed by the buyer and seller stating the terms and conditions under which a property will be sold.

Qualifying Ratios: Guidelines applied by the lenders to determine how large a loan to grant a home buyer.

Radon: A radioactive gas found in some homes that in sufficient concentrations can cause health problems.

Rate Lock: A written agreement guaranteeing the home buyer a specified interest rate provided the loan is closed within a set period of time. The lock-in also usually specifies the number of points to be paid at closing. Also known as Lock-In.

Real Estate Agent: A person licensed to negotiate and transact the sale of real estate on behalf of the property owner.

Real Estate Settlement Procedures Act (RESPA): A consumer protection law that requires lenders to give borrowers advance notice of closing costs.

Realtor: A collective membership mark that may be used only by real estate professionals who are members of the National Association of Realtors and subscribe to its strict code of ethics.

Refinancing: The process of paying off one loan with the proceeds from a new loan using the same property as security.

Reverse Mortgage: Also called "equity conversion mortgage", these loans permit senior citizens to convert the equity in their homes to income. The lender makes monthly cash payments to the homeowner, and repayment is deferred for a set period or until the homeowner dies and the house is sold.

Second Mortgage: A mortgage that has a lien position subordinate to the first mortgage.

Secondary Market: The buying and selling of existing mortgages.

Seller Take-Back: An agreement in which the owner of a property provides financing, often in combination with an assumed mortgage.

Settlement: The meeting at which a sale of a property is finalized by the buyer signing the mortgage documents and paying closing cost. Also known as "closing".

Settlement Sheet: The computation of costs payable at closing that determines the seller's net proceeds and the buyer's net payment.

Survey: A drawing or map showing the precise legal boundaries of a property, the location of improvements, easements, rights of way, encroachments, and other physical features.

Tenancy by Entirety: A type of joint ownership of property that provides right of survivorship and is available only to a husband and wife.

Tenancy in Common: A type of joint ownership in a property without right of survivorship.

Title: A legal document evidencing a person's right to or ownership of a property.

Title Company: A company that specializes in examining and insuring titles to real estate.

Title Insurance: Insurance to protect the lender (lender's policy) or the buyer (owner's policy) against loss arising from disputes over ownership of property.

Title Search: A check of the title records to ensure that the seller is the legal owner of the property and that there are no liens or other claims outstanding.

Treasury Securities: Treasury securities and T-Bills are common indexes for adjustable rate mortgages (ARMS).

Truth-In-Lending (TIL): A federal law that requires lenders to fully disclose, in writing, the terms and conditions of a mortgage including the "annual percentage rate APR)" and other charges.

Underwriting: The process of evaluating a loan application to determine the risk involved for the lender. It involves an analysis of the borrower's creditworthiness and the quality of the property itself.

VA Loan: A loan that is guaranteed by the Department of Veterans Affairs. Also referred to as a "government" mortgage.

<u>NOTES</u>

NOTES

NOTES

NOTES

Chapter 7

Real Estate Forms

On the following pages, I put in several forms different that I thought would be useful in your real estate endeavor and these forms are not copyrighted so, you may copy them or re-produce them on your computer.

ASSIGNMENT OF LEASE BY LESSEE
WITH CONSENT OF LESSOR

This Assignment made _____, 20__, by _____, of _____, as assignor, to _____of _____, as assignee.

For value received, assignor assigns and transfers to assignee that lease, dated _____, 20__, executed by assignor as lessee and by _____of _____, as lessor, of the following described premises, subject to all the conditions and terms contained in the lease, to have and to hold from _____, 20__, until the present term of the lease expires on _____, 20__. A copy of the lease is attached hereto and made a part hereof by reference.

Assignor covenants that he is the lawful and sole owner of the interest assigned hereunder, that this interest is free form all encumbrances: and that he ahs performed all duties and obligations and made all payments required under the terms and conditions of the lease.

Assignee agrees to pay all rent due after the effective date of this assignment, and to assume and perform all duties and obligations required by the terms of the lease.

_____Assignor

_____Assignee

CONSENT OF LESSOR

I, _____, lessor named in the above assignment of that lease executed by me on _____, 20__, consent to that assignment. I also consent to the agreement by assignee to assume after _____, 20__, the payment of rent and performance of all duties and obligations as set forth in the lease, and release _____, ;lessee and assignor, form all duties and obligations under the lease, including the payment of rent, after _____, 20__, and accept assignee as lessee in the place of _____, lessee and assignor.

Dated _____, 20__.

_____

CONTRACT EMPLOYING REAL ESTATE BROKER FOR LEASE OF PROPERTY

This agreement dated _____, is made By and Between _____, whose address is _____, referred to as "Owner", AND _____, whose address is _____, referred to as "Broker."

1. Property. Owner is the owner of the following real estate:

2. Employment of Broker. Owner gives the Broker the sole right to rent space in the above property to prospective tenants.

3. Commission. Owner agrees to pay the Broker a commission of ___DOLLARS ($_____) for services in obtaining the tenants and in negotiating and closing each lease. Owner reserves the right to reject any such lease and will not be responsible for any commission unless and until Owner accepts the lease and receive payment therefore. A commission of ___ DOLLARS ($____) will be payable for renewals of lease originally obtained by the Broker. All commissions will be paid out of rents received.

4. Sole Agency. I agree to refer all inquiries from prospective tenants or their agents to the Broker. The Broker agrees to use his or her best efforts to lease the property to such prospects.

5. Other Brokers. The Broker agrees to obtain the assistance of other brokers, as required, and to pay same out of the aforesaid commissions provided for in this agreement. In no event shall Owner be liable for additional commissions due to the efforts of any other broker.

6. Advertisement. The Broker and all other brokers as noted above shall be entitled to advertise the rental of this property and take all necessary steps in accordance with this agreement.

7. Signs. The Broker will provide suitable sign or signs to be placed on the property, subject to my approval.

8. Term of Agreement. This agreement shall remain effective until _____, unless terminated prior thereto.

9. Termination. Either party may terminate this contract on twenty (20) days notice. Such termination shall not limit the Brokers right to commissions resulting form pending negotiations and pending leases. However, no commissions shall be paid from rents received three (3) months after the termination of this agreement.

10. Signatures. Both the Broker and Owner agree to the above:

Witnessed by:_____"OWNER"

_____"BROKER"

AGREEMENT FOR EXTENSION OF LEASE

This Agreement is made and entered in this ___day of _____,20__, between _____, of _____,of _____, hereinafter referred to as "Landlord" and _____, of _____, hereinafter referred to as "Tenant" regarding the premises of Landlord generally located at _____and leased to Tenant under a lease dated _____, the term of which is to expire _____.

Now, therefore, it is agreed as follows:

1. The above-described lease is hereby renewed for a term of _____ beginning _____ and ending _____.

2. All terms, provisions and covenants of the above-described lease shall remain in full force for the duration of the extended term, except as noted.

3. In connection with this renewal, the rent, payable monthly, shall be $_____per month.

IN WITNESS WHEREOF, the parties hereto have executed this Agreement on the date first above written.

_____

_____

PERMISSION TO SUBLET

OWNER/Management _____

Premises _____

Resident_____

Date of Lease_____

1. Permission is hereby granted to the above-named resident to sublease the premises described above to _____for a term of _____, beginning_____ and ending _____.

2. Any and all subtenants shall be required to conform to all obligations and covenants of the resident as set forth in the above-described lease, all provisions of said lease remaining in full force an defect for the entire time of the sublease.

3. Any and all adult tenants shall be required to complete the landlord's standard rental application and must meet the usual character, employment, and credit requirements for tenancy, and pay landlord the required rental application fee and credit check fee.

4. In the event legal action is required to enforce any provision of this agreement, the prevailing party shall be entitled to recover reasonable attorney fees and costs.

5. This permission to sublet in no way releases the above-named resident from any obligation, responsibility or duty of the resident as set forth in the above-described lease.

IN WITNESS WHEREOF, the parties hereto have executed this agreement.

_____

Owner/Management

_____

Resident

NOTICE OF OVERDUE RENT

To: _____
_____
_____
_____

Your rent of $_____for the period of _____has not been received as of the above date.

Please be reminded that your rent was due on _____. Also, our lease agreement provides for a late charge of _____.

Your rent, including applicable late charges, should be sent to:

_____
_____
_____
_____

BY_____
OWNER/Management

Phone _____

PROPERTY MANAGEMENT AGREEMENT

Property Management Agreement

This Agreement is made and entered in the ____day of _____,20__, between _____, of _____, hereinafter called "Owner", and _____, of _____, hereinafter called "Manager".

Owner hereby employs the services of the Manager to manage, operate, control, rent and lease the following property:

Responsibilities of Manager

The Owner hereby appoints Manager as his lawful agent and attorney-in-fact with full authority to do any and all lawful things necessary for the fulfillment of this Agreement, including the following:

1. To collect all rents due and as they became due, giving receipts therefore; to render to the Owner a monthly accounting of rents received and expenses paid out; and to remit to the Owner all income, less any sums paid out.

2. To make or cause to be made all decorating, maintenance, alterations and repairs to said property and to hire and supervise all employees and other labor for the accomplishment of same.

3. To advertise the property and display signs thereon; to rent and lease the property; to sign, renew and cancel rental agreements and leases for the property or any part thereof; to sue and recover for rent and for loss of or damage to any part of the property and/or furnishings thereof, and, when expedient, to compromise, settle and release any such legal proceedings or lawsuits.

Liability of Manager

Owner hereby agrees to hold Manager harmless from any an d all claims, charges, debts, demands and lawsuits, including attorney's fees related to his management of the herein-described property, and from any liability for injury on or about the property which may be suffered by any employee, tenant or guest upon the property.

Compensation of Manager

Owner agrees to compensate Manager as follows:

Term of Agreement

The term of the Agreement shall commence on the ___day of _____, 20___, and end on the _____day of _____,20___.

Upon expiration of the above initial term, this Agreement shall automatically be renewed and extended for a like period of time unless terminated in writing by either party 30 days prior to the date for such renewal.

This Agreement may also be terminated by mutual agreement of the parties at any time upon payment to Manager of all fees, commission and expenses due Manager under terms of this Agreement.

Extent of Agreement

This document represents the entire Agreement between the parties hereto.

IN WITNESS WHEREOF, the parties hereto herby execute this Agreement on the date first above written.

_____

_____

LEASE AGREEMENT FOR FURNISHED HOUSE

This Agreement is made and entered in this _____day of _____,
20___, between _____, of _____,
hereinafter referred to as "Landlord" and _____, of
_____, hereinafter referred to as "Tenant".

WHEREAS, Landlord desires to lease to Tenant and Tenant desires to lease
from Landlord the premises generally described as _____, it
is herein agreed as follows:

1. Landlord hereby leases to Tenant, the furnished premises described above
for a term of ____beginning _____and ending _____, at a
monthly rate of $_____.

2. The described premises are leased furnished, to include all furnishes enumerated on the list of Furnishings, which is a part of this lease, signed by both
parties and dated.

3. Tenant agrees to pay the rent herein provided subject to the terms and conditions set forth herein.

4. Rent shall be payable in equal monthly installments on the ___day of each
month, to the address of Landlord as stated above or at such other address as
Landlord may, from time to time, require.

5. Tenant shall pay for all electricity, water, fuel oil and gas during the term of
this lease and an extension or renewal thereof.

6. Landlord covenants that the leased premises are, to the best of his knowledge, clean, safe, sound and healthful and that there exists no violation of any
applicable housing code, law or regulation of which he is aware.

7. Tenant agrees to comply with all sanitary laws, ordinances and rules affecting the cleanliness, occupancy and preservation of the premises during the
term of this lease.

8. Tenant shall use the leased premises exclusively for a private residence for occupancy by no more than ____persons, unless otherwise specified herein, and Tenant shall not make any alterations to the house, outbuildings or grounds without written consent of Landlord.

9. Tenant shall keep the premises in good order and repair and shall advise Landlord or Landlord's agent of any needed repairs and maintenance reasonably expected to cost $_____or more.

10. Tenant agrees to take good care of the furniture, carpets, draperies, appliances and other household goods, and the personal effects of Landlord, and further agrees that he will deliver up same to Landlord in good condition at the end of the term of this lease, normal wear and tear expected.

11. Tenant shall repair or replace, a t Tenant's expense, all loss or damage to any of the listed furniture, carpets, draperies, appliances and other household goods, and personal effects of Landlord, whenever such damage or loss shall have resulted from Tenant's misuse, waste or neglect of said furnishings and personal effects of Landlord.

12. Tenant shall cause to be made, at Tenant's expense, all required repairs to heating and air-conditioning apparatus, electric and gas fixtures and plumbing work whenever such damage shall have resulted from misuse, waste or neglect of Tenant, it being understood that Landlord is to have same in good order and repair when giving possession.

13. Tenant shall not keep or have in or on the leased house, outbuildings or grounds any article or thing of a dangerous, flammable or explosive nature that might be pronounced "hazardous: or extra hazardous: by any responsible insurance company.

14. Tenant shall give prompt notice to Landlord or his agent of any dangerous, defective, unsafe or emergency condition in or on the leased premises, said notice being by any suitable means. Landlord or his agent shall repair and correct said conditions promptly upon receiving notice thereof from Tenant.

15. Landlord covenants that the Tenant and Tenant's family shall have, hold and enjoy the leased premises for the term of this lease, subject to the conditions set froth herein.

16. Tenant covenants that he shall not commit nor permit a nuisance in or upon the premises, that he shall not maliciously or by reason of gross negligence damage the house, outbuildings or grounds, and that he shall not engage, nor permit any member of his family to engage, in conduct so as to interfere substantially with the comfort and safety of residents of adjacent buildings.

17. Tenant agrees to place a security deposit with Landlord in the amount of $____, to be used by Landlord at the termination of this lease for the cost of replacing or repairing damage, if any, to the house, outbuildings, grounds, furnishings or personal effects of Landlord resulting from the intentional or negligent acts of Tenant.

18. Landlord agrees to return said security deposit to Tenant within ten says of the Tenant's vacating the leased premises subject to the terms and conditions set forth herein.

19. Tenant shall, at reasonable times, give access to Landlord or his agents for any reasonable and lawful purpose. Except in situations of compelling emergency, Landlord or his agents shall give the Tenant at least 24 hours' notice of intention to seek access, the date and time at which access will be sought, and the reason therefore.

20. In the event of default by Tenant, Tenant shall remain liable for all rent due or to become due during the term of this lease. Landlord or his agents shall have the obligation to relet the premises in the Landlord's name for the balance of the term, or longer, and will apply proceeds of such reletting toward the reduction of Tenant's obligations enumerated herein.

21. Tenant shall permit Landlord or his agents to show the premises at reasonable hours, to persons desiring to rent or purchase same, 30 days prior to the expiration of this lease, and will permit the notice "To Let" or "For Sale" to be placed on said premises and remain thereon without hindrance or molestation after said date.

22. In the event of any breach by the Tenant of any of Tenant's covenants or agreements herein, Landlord or his agents may give Tenant five days' notice to cure said breach, setting forth in writing which covenants or agreements have been breached. If any breach is not cured within said five-day period, or reasonable steps to effectuate said cure are not commenced and diligently pursued within said five-day period and thereafter until said breach has been cured, Landlord or his agents may terminate this lease upon five days' additional notice

to the Tenant, with said notice being in lieu of a Notice to Quit, which Tenant hereby waives.

23. In the event of any breach by Landlord of any of Landlord's covenants or agreements herin, Tenant may give Landlord ten days' notice to cure said breach, setting forth in writing the manner in which said covenants and agreements have been breached. If said breach is not cured within said ten-day period, or reasonable steps to effectuate said cure are not commenced and diligently pursued within said ten-day period and thereafter until said breach has been cured, rent hereunder shall be fully abated from the time at which said ten days' notice expired until such time as Landlord has fully cured the breach set forth in the notice provided for in this paragraph.

24. In no case shall any abatement of rent hereunder be effected where the condition set forth in the notice provided for herein was created by the intentional or negligent act of the Tenant, but Landlord shall have the burden of proving that rent abatement may not be effected for the foregoing reason.

25. Landlord agrees to deliver possession of the leased premises at the beginning of the term provided for herein. In the event of Landlord's failure to deliver possession at the beginning of said term, Tenant shall have the right to rescind this lease and recover any consideration paid under terms of this Agreement.

26. Tenant agrees that this lease shall be subject to and subordinate to any mortgage or mortgages now on said premises or which any owner of said premises may hereafter at any time elect to place on said premises.

27. Unless otherwise provided for elsewhere in this lease, any notice required or authorized herein shall be given in writing, one copy of said notice mailed via U.S. certified mail, return receipt requested, and one copy of said notice mailed via U.S. first-class mail.

Notice to Tenant shall be mailed to him at the leased premises. Notice to Landlord shall be mailed to him, or to the managing agent, at their respective addresses as set forth herein, or at such new address as to which the Tenant has been duly notified.

28. This lease constitutes the entire agreement between the parties hereto. No changes shall be made herein except by writing, signed by each party and dated. The failure to enforce any right or remedy hereunder, and the payment

and acceptance of rent hereunder, shall not be deemed a waiver by either party of such right or remedy in the absence of a writing as provided for herein.

29. In the event legal action is required to enforce any provision of this Agreement, the prevailing party shall be entitled to recovery reasonable attorney's fees and costs.

30. Landlord and Tenant agree that this lease, when filled out and signed, is a binging legal obligation.

IN WITNESS WHEREOF, the parties hereto have executed this Agreement on the date first above written.

_____

_____

RENT RECEIPT

Date: _____
TO: Tenant _____ Unit Address _____
Received from _____ the sum of $ _____, which
is rent for the period of _____ for the premises
described above.
LANDLORD

_____

RENT RECEIPT

Date: _____
TO: Tenant _____ Unit Address _____
Received from _____ the sum of $ _____, which
is rent for the period of _____ for the premises
described above.
LANDLORD

_____

RENT RECEIPT

Date: _____
TO: Tenant _____ Unit Address _____
Received from _____ the sum of $ _____, which
is rent for the period of _____ for the premises
described above.
LANDLORD

_____

LEASE AGREEMENT

Lease Agreement

THIS LEASE AGREEMENT (hereinafter referred to as the "Agreement") made and entered into this ___ day of _____, 20 ___, by and between _____, whose address is _____ (hereinafter referred to as "Lessor") and _____ (hereinafter referred to as "Lessee")

W I T N E S S E T H:

WHEREAS, Lessor is the fee owner of certain real property being, lying and situate in _____County, _____, such real property having a street address of _____.

WHEREAS, Lessor is desirous of leasing the Premises from Lessor on the terms and conditions as contained herein;

NOW, THEREFORE, for and in consideration of the sum of TEN DOLLARS ($10.00), the covenants and obligations contained herein and other good and valuable consideration, the receipt and sufficiency of which is hereby acknowledged, the parties hereto hereby agree as follows:

1. TERM. Lessor leases to Lessee and Lessee leases from Lessor the above described Premises together with any and all appurtenances thereto, for a term of ___ year(s), such term beginning on _____. And ending at 12 o'clock midnight on _____.

2. RENT. The total rent for the term hereof is the sum of _____ DOLLARS ($_____) payable on the ___day of each month of the term, in equal installments of _____DOLLARS ($_____) first and last installments to be paid upon the due execution of the Agreement, the second installment to be paid on _____. All such payments shall be made to Lessor at Lessor's address as set forth in the preamble to this Agreement on or before the due date and without demand.

3. DAMAGE DEPOSIT. Upon the due execution of this Agreement, Lessee shall deposit with Lessor the sum of _____ DOLLARS ($_____) receipt of which is hereby acknowledged by Lessor, as security

for any damage caused to the Premises during the term hereof. Such deposit shall be returned to Lessee, without interest, and less any set off for damages to the Premises upon the termination of this Agreement.

4. USE OF PREMISES. The Premises shall be used and occupied by Lessee and Lessee's immediate family, consisting of part of the Premises shall be used at any time during the term of this Agreement by Lessee for the purpose of carrying on any business, profession, or trade of any kind, or for any purpose other than as a private single family dwelling. Lessee shall not allow any other person, other than Lessee's immediate family or transient relatives and friends who are guests of Lessee shall not allow any other person, other than Lessee's immediate family or transient relatives and friends who are guests of Lessee to use or occupy the Premises without fist obtaining Lessor's written consent to such use. Lessee shall comply with any and all laws, ordinances, rules and orders of any and all governmental or quasi-governmental authorities affecting the cleanliness, use occupancy and preservation of the Premises.

5. CONDITION OF PREMISES. Lessee stipulates, represents and warrants that Lessee has examined the Premises, and that they are at the time of this Lease in good order, repair, and in a safe, clean and tenantable condition.

6. ASSIGNMENT AND SUB-LETTING. Lessee shall not assign this Agreement, or sub-let or grant any license to use the Premises or any part thereof without the prior written consent of Lessor. Consent by Lessor to one such assignment, sub-letting or license shall not be deemed to be a consent to any subsequent assignment, sub-letting or license. An assignment, sub-letting or license without the prior written consent of Lessor or an assignment or sub-letting by operation of law shall be absolutely null and void and shall, at Lessor's option, terminate this Agreement.

7. ALTERATIONS AND IMORIVEMENTS. Lessee shall make no alterations to the buildings or improvements on the Premises or construct any building or make any other improvements on the Premises without the prior written consent of Lessor. Any and all alterations, changes, and/or improvements built, constructed or placed on the Premises by Lessee shall, unless otherwise provided by written agreement between Lessor and lessee, be and become the property of Lessor and remain on the Premises at the expiration or earlier termination of this Agreement.

8. NON-DELIVERY OF POSSESSION. In the event Lessor cannot deliver possession of the Premises to Lessee upon the commencement of the Lease term, through no fault of Lessor or its agents, then Lessor or its agents shall have no liability, but the rental herein provided shall abate until possession is give, Lessor or its agents shall have thirty (30) days in which to give possession, and if possession is tendered within such time, Lessee agrees to accept the demised Premises and pay the rental herein provided from that date. In the event possession cannot be delivered within such time, through no fault of Lessor or its agents, then this Agreement and all rights hereunder shall terminate.

9. HAZARDOUS MATERIALS. Lessee shall not keep on the Premises any item of a dangerous, flammable or explosive character that might unreasonably increase the danger of fire or explosion on the Premises or that might be considered hazardous or extra hazardous by any responsible insurance company.

10. UTILITIES. Lessee shall be responsible for arranging for and paying for all utility services required on the Premises.

11. MAINTENANCE AND REPAIR; RULES. Lessee will, at its sole expense, keep and maintain the Premises and appurtenances in good and sanitary condition and repair during the term of this Agreement and any renewal thereof. Without limiting the generality of the foregoing, Lessee shall:

(a) Not obstruct the driveways, sidewalks, courts, entry ways, stairs and/or halls, which shall be used for the purposes of ingress and egress only;

(b) Keep all windows, glass, window coverings, doors, locks and hardware in good, clean order and repair;

(c) Not obstruct or cover the windows or door'

(d) Not leave windows or doors in an open position during an inclement weather;

(e) Not hang any laundry, clothing, sheets, etc. from any window, rail, porch, or balcony nor air or dry any of same within any yard area or space;

(f) Not cause or permit any locks or hooks to be placed upon any door or window without the prior written consent of Lessor;

(g) Keep all air conditioning filters clean and free from dirt;

(h) Keep all lavatories, sinks, toilets, and all other water and plumbing apparatus in good order and repair and shall use same only for the purposes for which they were constructed. Lessee shall not allow any sweepings, rubbish, sand, rages, ashes or other substances to be thrown or deposited therein. Any damage to any such apparatus and the cost of clearing stopped plumbing resulting from misuse shall be borne by Lessee;

(i) And Lessee's family and guests shall at all times maintain order in the Premises and at all places on the Premises, and shall not make or permit any loud or improper noises, or otherwise disturb other residents;

(j) Keep all radios, television sets, stereos, phonographs, etc., turned down to a level of sound that does not annoy or interfere with other residents;

(k) Deposit all trash, garbage, rubbish or refuse in the locations provided therefore and shall not allow any trash, garbage, rubbish or refuse to be deposited or permitted to stand on the exterior of any building or within the common elements;

(l) Abide by and be bound by any and all rules and regulations affecting the Premises or the common area appurtenant thereto which may be adopted or promulgated by the Condominium or Homeowners' Association having control over them.

12. DAMAGE TO PREMISES. In the event the Premises are destroyed or rendered wholly untenantable by fire, storm, earthquake, or other casualty not caused by the negligence of Lessee, this Agreement shall terminate from such time except for the purpose of enforcing rights that may have then accrued hereunder. The rental provided for herein shall then be accounted for by and between Lessor and Lessee up to the time of such injury or destruction of the Premises, Lessee paying rentals up to such date and Lessor refunding rentals collected beyond such date. Should a portion of the Premises thereby be rendered untenantable, the Lessor shall have the option of either repairing such injured or damaged portion or terminating this Lease. In the event that Lessor exercises its right to repair such untenantable portion, the rental shall abate in the proportion that the injured parts bears to the whole Premises, and such part so injured shall be restored by Lessor as speedily as practicable, after which the full rent shall recommence and the Agreement continue according to its terms.

13. INSPECTION OF PREMISES. Lessor and Lessor's agents shall have the right at all reasonable times during the term of this Agreement and any renewal thereof to enter the Premises for the purpose of inspecting the Premises and al buildings and improvements thereon. And for the purposes of making any repairs, additions or alterations as may be deemed appropriate by Lessor for the preservation of the Premises or the building. Lessor and its agents shall further have the right to exhibit the Premises and to display the usual "for sale", "for rent" or "vacancy" signs on the Premises at any time within forty-five (45) days before the expiration of this Lease. The right of entry shall likewise exist for the purpose of removing placards, signs, fixtures, alterations or additions, but do not conform to this Agreement or to any restrictions, rules or regulations affecting the Premises.

14. SUBORINATION OF LEASE. This Agreement and Lessee's interest here-under are and shall be subordinate, junior and inferior to any and all mort-gages, liens, or encumbrances now or hereafter placed on the Premises by Lessor, all advances made under any such mortgages, liens or encumbrances (including, but not limited to, future advances), the interest payable on such mortgages, liens or encumbrances and any and all renewals, extensions or modifications of such mortgages, liens or encumbrances.

15. LESSEE'S HOLD OVER. If Lessee remains in possession of the Premises with the consent of Lessor after the natural expiration of this Agreement, a new tenancy from month-to-month shall be created between Lessor and Lessee which shall be subject to all of the terms and conditions hereof except that rent shall then be due and owing at _____ DOLLARS ($_____) per month and except that such tenancy shall be terminable upon fifteen (15) days written notice served by either party.

16. SURRENDER OF PREMISES. Upon the expiration of the term hereof, Lessee shall surrender the Premises in as good a state and condition as they were at the commencement of this Agreement, reasonable use and wear and tear thereof and damages by the elements excepted.

17. ANIMALS. Lessee shall be entitled to keep no more than ___ (___) domes-tic dogs, cats or birds; however, at such time as Lessee shall actually keep any such animal on the Premises, Lessee shall pay to Lessor a pet deposit of _____ DOLLARS ($_____), _____ DOLLARS ($_____) of which shall be non-refundable and shall be used upon the

termination or expiration of this Agreement for the purposes of cleaning the carpets of the building.

18. QUIET ENJOYMENT. Lessee, upon payment of all of the sums referred to herein as being payable by Lessee and Lessee's performance of all Lessee's agreements contained herein and Lessee's observance of all rules and regulations, shall and may peacefully and quietly have, hold and enjoy said Premises for the term hereof.

19. INDEMNIFICATION. Lessor shall not be liable for any damage or injury of or to the Lessee, Lessee's family, guests, invitees, agents or employees or to any person entering the Premises or the building of which the Premises are a part or to goods or equipment, or in the structure of equipment of the structure of which the Premises are a part, and Lessee hereby agrees to indemnify, defend and hold Lessor harmless from any and all claims to assertions of every kind and nature.

20. DEFAULT. If Lessee fails to comply with any of the material provisions of this Agreement, other than the covenant to pay rent, or of any present rules and regulation or any that may be hereafter prescribed by Lessor, or materially fails to comply with any duties imposed on Lessee by stature, within seven (7) days after delivery of written notice by Lessor specifying the non-compliance and indicating the intention of Lessor to terminate the Lease by reason thereof, Lessor may terminate this Agreement.

If Lessee fails to pay rent when due and the default continues for seven (7) days thereafter, Lessor may, at Lessor's option, declare the entire balance of rent payable hereunder to be immediately due and payable and may exercise any and all rights and remedies available to Lessor at law or in equity or may immediately terminate this Agreement.

21. LATE CHARGES. In the event that any payment required to be paid by lessee hereunder is not made within three (3) days of when due, Lessee shall pay to Lessor, in addition to such payment or other charges due hereunder, a "late fee" in the amount of _____ ($_____)

22. ABANDONMENT. If at any time during the term of this Agreement Lessee abandons the Premises or any part thereof, Lessor may, at Lessor's option, obtain possession of the Premises in the manner provided by law, and without becoming liable to Lessee for damages or for any payment of any kind whatever. Lessor may, at Lessor's discretion, as agent for Lessee, relet the Premises,

or any part thereof, for the whole of any part thereof, for the whole or any part of the then unexpired term, and may receive and collect all rent payable by virtue of such reletting, and at Lessor's option, hold Lessee liable for any difference between the rent that would have been payable under this Agreement during the balance of the unexpired term, if this Agreement had continued in force, and the net rent for such period realized by Lessor by means of such reletting. If Lessor's right of reentry is exercised following abandonment of the Premises by Lessee, the Lessor shall consider nay personal property belonging to Lessee and left on the Premises to also have been abandoned, in which case Lessor may dispose of all property belonging to Lessee and left on the Premises to also have been abandoned, in which case Lessor may dispose of all such personal property in any manner Lessor shall deem proper and Lessor is hereby relieved of all liability for doing so.

23. ATTORNEY'S FEES. Should it become necessary for Lessor to employ an attorney to enforce any of the conditions or covenants hereof, including the collection of rentals or gaining possession of the Premises, Lessee agrees to pay all expenses so incurred, including a reasonable attorneys' fee.

24. RECORDING OF AGREEMENT. Lessee shall not record this Agreement on the Public Records of any public office. In the event that Lessee shall record this Agreement, this Agreement shall, at Lessor's option, terminate immediately and Lessor shall be entitled to all rights and remedies that it has at law or in equity.

25. GOVERNING LAW. This Agreement shall be governed, construed and interpreted by, through and under the Laws of the State of _____.

26. SEVERABILITY. If any provision of this Agreement or the application thereof shall, for any reason and to any extent, be invalid or unenforceable, neither the remainder of this Agreement nor the application of the provision to other persons, entities or circumstances shall be affected thereby, but instead shall be enforced to the maximum extent permitted by law.

27. BINDING EFFECT. The covenants, obligations and conditions herein contained shall be binding on and inure to the benefit of the heirs, legal representatives, and assigns of the parties hereto.

28. DESCRIPTIVE HEADING. The descriptive headings used herein are for convenience of reference only and they are not intended to have any effect whatsoever in determining the rights or obligations of the Lessor or Lessee.

29. CONSTRUCTION. The pronouns used herein shall include, where appropriate, either gender or both, singular and plural.

30. NON-WAIVER. No indulgence, waiver, election or non-election by Lessor under this Agreement shall affect Lessee's duties and liabilities hereunder.

31. MODIFICATION. The parties hereby agree that this document contains the entire agreement between the parties and this Agreement shall not be modified, changed, altered or amended in any way except through a written amendment signed by all of the parties hereto.

IN WITNESS WHEREOF, the parties have caused these presents to be duly executed:

As to Lessor this ____day of _____, 20____.

Witnesses: "Lessor"

_____

_____

_____

As to Lessee this ____day of _____, 20____.

Witnesses: "Lessee"

_____

_____

_____

RENTAL APPLICATION

Date: _____

Application is hereby made to rent premises generally described as _____ for a term of _____ and ending the _____day of _____, 20___, for which monthly rental shall be $_____, payable in advance, and for which a security deposit of $_____ shall be due prior to occupancy of the above-described premises.

A deposit of $_____ is made herewith on account of the first month's rent, with the understanding that if this application is accepted and the applicant fails to execute a lease before the beginning date specified above, or to pay the balance due as first month's rent, said payment will be forfeited as liquidated damages.

It is also understood that if this application is not accepted or if the premises are not ready for occupancy by the applicant on the date specified above, said deposit shall be refunded to the applicant forthwith, upon applicant's request.

APPLICANT

Name: _____

Present Address: _____ How Long? _____
Previous Address: _____ How Long? _____
Married: _____ Spouse's Name: _____
Children? _____ How Many? _____ Ages? _____
Pets? _____ What Kind? _____ How Many? _____

YOUR EMPLOYMENT

Employer: _____
Employer Address: _____
Supervisor: _____ Bus. Phone_____
How Long on Present Job? _____ Annual Income: _____

SPOUSE'S EMPLOYMENT

Employer: _____

Employer Address: _____

Supervisor: _____ Bus. Phone: _____

How Long on Present Job? _____ Annual Income: _____

REFERENCES

Bank: _____ Phone: _____

Personal Reference: _____ Phone: _____

Credit Reference: _____ Phone: _____

Credit Reference: _____ Phone: _____

_____The information provided herein may be used by the landlord or his agent to determine whether to accept this application. Upon written request within 30 days the landlord or his agent will disclose to applicant in writing the nature and scope of any investigation landlord has requested, and will, if this application is refused, state in writing the reason for said refusal.

Accepted _____ Refused _____

MONTH TO MONTH RENTAL AGREEMENT

Date: _____, 20___

RECEIPT IS HEREBY ACKNOWLEDGED by _____
hereinafter   Called   Management,   from
_____ hereinafter called Resident, the sum
of $_____ for the first month's rent of the premises owned by said
Management and located at _____ hereinafter
called premises, said premises he Management herby agrees to rent to said
Resident on a month-to-month basis at a rental of $_____per
month, payable in advance on the ____day of each and every succeeding cal-
endar month.

In considered hereof and of the use or occupancy of the said premises,
Resident agrees:

1. TO maintain said premises in a clean, orderly, and law abiding manner and
to keep the yards thereof free of weeds, debris, and/or material that may
become unsightly or a detriment to the appearance of said premises.
Management shall have the right to enter and inspect said premises at any and
all reasonable times.

2. No alterations or redecorating of any kind to the dwelling shall be made
without the prior written consent of Management.

3. To pay for all utility service furnished to the property.

4. To pay the cost of all repairs for any damage done to said premises and the
cost of any cleaning up of said premises which Management may consider necessary.

5. No birds, animals, or other pets shall be kept on the premises without the
knowledge and written consent form management; any consent, so given may
be withdrawn, if, in the opinion of Management, such bird, animal, or other
pet constitutes a nuisance, causes complaint from neighbors, or adversely
affects the normal maintenance of the property.

6. Not to let or sublet the whole or any part of the premises to anyone for any
purpose whatsoever without prior written permission form Management, and

the number of persons to occupy said premises shall not exceed without written permission from Management.

7. To give thirty days written notice by registered mail to Management prior to vacating said premises and to permit prospective tenants the opportunity of reasonable inspection.

8. To clean up said premises upon vacating and restore said premises to the same condition they are now in, reasonable wear and tear and damage by the elements excepted.

9. That the violation of any of the covenants of this agreement or the nonpayment of any rent due and unpaid shall be sufficient cause for eviction from said premises upon three (3) days written notice thereof by registered mail or by personal service. If suit be brought to collect rent or damages, to cause eviction from said premises, or to collect the costs of repairs to or cleaning of said premises, Resident agrees to pay all costs of such action, including reasonable attorney fees as may be fixed by the Court. No waiver by Management at any time of any of the terms of this agreement shall be deemed as a subsequent waiver of the same, nor of the strict and prompt performance thereof by the Resident.

10. All rent shall be paid at the office of _____,
or any other place designated by Management. Each party hereto acknowledges receipt of a copy of this agreement.

_____ Signed

_____

Management Resident

By _____ Signed

_____

Resident

LANDLORD'S FIVE DAY NOTICE

To: _____

You are hereby notified that there is now due to the undersigned landlord the sum of _____ dollars being rent for the premises located in _____, County of _____, and state of _____. Described as follows: _____
_____
_____

And you are further notified that payment of said sum so due has been and is hereby demanded of you, and that unless payment thereof is made on or before the expiration of five (5) days after service of this notice, your lease of said premises will be terminated.

Only FULL PAYMENT of the rent demanded in this notice will waive the landlord's right to terminate the lease under this notice, unless the landlord agrees, in writing, to continue the lease in exchange for receiving partial payment.

Dated this ___day of _____, 20_____.
_____
Landlord/Managing Agent Address

_____
Telephone

_____
STATE OF _____AFFIDAVIT OF SERVICE—When served by a person not an officer.

COUNTY OF _____,
being duly sworn, on oath deposes and says that on the ____day of _____, 20___ he/she served the within notice on the tenant named as follows: *

_____ (1) by delivering a copy thereof to the within named tenant, _____.

_____ (2) by delivering a copy thereof to _____, person above the age of ten years, residing in or in charge of the within described premises.

_____ (3) by sending a copy thereof to said tenant by **registered/certified mail, return receipt requested.

_____ (4) by posting a copy thereof on the main door of the within described premises, no on being in actual possession thereof.

*Check off all applicable paragraphs.

_____

**Strike out word not applicable. Signature of Notice Server

Subscribed and sworn to before me this __day of _____, 20___

(Seal)

_____

Notary Public

LEASE

Lease

This lease of _____, made _____, by and
between_____, whose address is _____, hereinafter called Lessor, and _____, whose address is
_____, hereinafter called Lessee,

Witnesseth:

1. That Lessor hereby leases to Lessee, and Lessee leases from Lessor, subject to the terms and conditions herein set forth, the following (hereinafter sometimes referred to as the "Property"):

Make and Model Manufacturer's Serial No. Registration No

Together with all equipment and accessories attached thereto or used in connection therewith including the following: _____

All of which are included in the term Property as used herein. Lessee hereby acknowledges delivery and acceptance of the aforesaid Property upon the terms and conditions of this lease.

2. Lessor hereby lease to Lessee said Property for the purpose of _____.

3. The term of this lease is _____, beginning this day and ending _____.

4. In consideration of said lease, Lessee covenants and agrees as follows:

(a) To pay to Lessor for the possession and use of said Property for the purpose aforesaid, _____dollars ($____), payable as follows: _____.

(b) To safely keep and carefully use the Property and not sell or attempt to sell, remove or attempt to remove, the same or any part thereof, except reasonably for the purpose aforesaid.

(c) Lessee shall, during the term of this lease and until return and delivery of the Property to Lessor, abide by and conform to, and cause others to abide by and conform to, all laws and governmental and airport orders, rules and regulations, including any future amendments thereto, controlling or in any manner affecting operation, use or occupancy of said Property or use of airport premises by said Property.

(d) Lessee shall pay all taxes, assessments and charges on said Property or its use during the time he is in possession of the same, imposed by federal, state, municipal or other public, or other authority; save Lessor free and harmless therefrom; and to these ends reimburse Lessor on a pro rata basis for such taxes or charges paid by Lessor hereto or hereafter.

(e) Lessee accepts the Property in its present condition, and during the term of this lease and until return and delivery of the Property Lessor the Lessee shall maintain it in its present condition, reasonable wear and tear occurring despite standards of good maintenance of Property excepted, and shall repair at his own expense any damages to said Property caused by operation or use by lessee or by others during the tem of this lease and until delivery of the Property to Lessor.

(f) Neither Lessee nor others shall have the right to incur any mechanic's or other lien in connection with the repair, maintenance or storage of said Property, and Lessee agrees that neither he nor others will attempt to convey or mortgage or create any lien of any kind or character against the same or do anything or take action that might mature into such a lien.

(g) Lessee shall be responsible and liable to Lessor for, and indemnify Lessor against, any and all damage to the Property, which occurs in any manner from any cause or causes during the term of this lease or until return and delivery of the Property to Lessor. Lessee shall be responsible and liable for, indemnify lessor against, hold Lessor free and harmless from any claim or claims of any kind whatsoever for or from, and promptly pay any judgment for, any and all liability for personal injuries, death or property damages, or any of them, which arise or in any manner are occasioned by the acts or negligence of Lessee or others in the custody, operation or use of, or with respect to, said Property, during the term of this lease or until return and delivery of the Property to Lessor.

(h) Lessee will keep insured from and including this day until return and delivery of the Property to Lessor, in such company or companies as Lessor shall approve, according to applicable standard forms of policy, and for the benefit of Lessor, (1) against loss or damage form any cause or causes to the Property for the full value thereof in the amount of one million dollars, and (2) against liability for personal injuries, death, or property damages, or any of them, arising or in any manner occasioned by the acts or negligence of Lessee or others in the custody, operation or use of, or with respect to said Property, in the amount of one million dollars relative to personal injuries and/or death and one million dollars relative to property damages.

(i) Lessee shall return and deliver, at the expiration of the term herein granted the whole of said Property to the Lessor in as good condition as the same is, reasonable wear and tear excepted.

(j) It is mutually agreed that in case Lessee shall violate any of the aforesaid covenants, terms and conditions Lessor may at his option without notice terminate this lease and take possession of said Property wherever found. WITNESSES

_____ LESSOR

_____

_____ LESSEE

_____

REAL ESTATE SALESMAN
INDEPENDENT CONTRACTOR AGREEMENT

THIS AGREEMENT made and entered into this ___ day of _____, 19___, by and between _____, of _____, (hereinafter referred to as "Broker"), and _____ of _____, (hereinafter referred to as "Salesman"). The Parties recite that:

A. Broker is duly registered and licensed with the State of _____ as a real estate broker whose license expires _____.

B. Salesman is duly registered and licensed with the State of _____ as a real estate salesman whose license expires _____.

In consideration of the mutual covenants set forth below, the parties agree as follows:

1. STATEMENT OF EMPLOYMENT

Effective as of the date of this Agreement, Broker employs Salesman as a real estate salesman.

2. DUTIES OF SALESMAN

Salesman will carry on the customary activities of a real estate salesman, including, but not necessarily limited to, the showing of parcels of real estate on which Broker has listings, the sale of such property in accordance with the terms of the listings, the solicitation of new listings, and such other services pertaining to the real estate business as Broker may require of him. Salesman shall devote his entire time and attention to such duties and shall use his best efforts with regard to all of such duties.

3. COMMISSIONS ON SALES

Broker shall pay to Salesman a commission equal to ___ percent of the total commission received by Broker, on sales made by Salesman and completed during the effective period of this Agreement. Furthermore, during the effective period of this Agreement, Broker will advance to Salesman against commissions to be earned the sum of _____ DOLLARS ($_____) per month, provided that Salesman may elect to draw commissions as earned.

4. DURATION OF AGREEMENT; TERMINATION

The term of this Agreement shall be for __ years, commencing on the date of this Agreement. Either party may terminate this Agreement by sixty (60) days' written notice to the other party. If, on termination of this Agreement, Broker has advanced to Salesman against commissions to be earned a sum of commissions actually earned by Salesman, Salesman will promptly refund the amount of the excess advances.

5. ACCESS TO LISTINGS AND OTHER INFORMATION

Broker will give Salesman access to its confidential files pertaining to listings of property, prospects for the sale of such property, and other related matters. Broker shall also furnish Salesman personal contacts with persons interested in selling or buying such property, and shall generally aid Salesman in every way possible with respect to such sales and Salesman's duties here under.

6. LOYALTY TO BROKER'S INTEREST

Salesman will not during the term of this Agreement be engaged in any other business activity, whether or not pursued for gain, profit, or other pecuniary advantage, provided, however, that Salesman may invest his assets in such form or manner as will not require his expenditure of any undue amount of time.

7. NONDISCLOSURE OF TRADE SECRETS

Salesman recognizes and acknowledges that the information that will be furnished to him concerning Broker's customers, listings, holdings, investments, transactions, and other confidential matters constitutes a valuable, special, and unique asset and trade secret of Broker's business. Accordingly, Salesman will not, during or after the term of his employment hereunder, disclose any such information or any part thereof to any person, firm, corporation, association, or other entity for any reason or purpose whatsoever.

8. WRITTEN CONTRACT AS CONSTITUTING ENTIRE AGREEMENT

This Agreement constitutes the entire contract and agreement between parties, and there are no verbal understandings or other agreements of any nature with respect to the subject matter hereof except those contained in this Agreement.

9. BINDING EFFECT

This Agreement shall be binding upon and inure to the benefit of the respective heirs, successors and assigns of the parties hereto.

10. GOVERNING LAW

This Agreement shall be governed, interpreted and construed by, through and under the laws of the state of _____.

11. ATTORNEYS' FEES

In the event of any legal or equitable action, including any appeals, which may arise hereunder between or among the parties hereto, the prevailing party shall be entitled to recover reasonable attorneys' fee. Attorneys' fees shall also include hourly charges for paralegal, law clerks and other staff members operating under the supervision of an attorney.

12. SEVERANCE

The invalidity or unenforceability of any portion of this Agreement shall not affect the remaining provisions and portions hereof.

13. HEADINGS

The paragraph headings contained herein are for convenience of reference only and are not to be used in the construction or interpretation hereof.

IN WITNESS WHEREOF, the parties have caused these presents to be duly executed on the date first above written.

WITNESSES:

"BROKER"

_____

"SALESMAN"

_____

ASSIGNMENT OF RENTS BY LESSOR
WITH REPURCHASE AGREEMENT

1. For value received, _____, of _____, assignor, assigns and transfers to _____, of _____, assignee, all rents and other sums due and to become due assignor under that lease dated _____, 20___, between assignor as lessor, and _____, as lessee, for the lease of the following described property: _____.

2. Assignor warrants and represents that:

a. Assignor is the lawful owner of the above—described lease and of the rental property that is the subject thereof and of all rights and interests therein;

b. The lease is genuine, valid, and enforceable;

c. Assignor has a right to make this assignment;

d. The rental property and rental payments and other sums are free from liens, encumbrances, claims and set offs of every kind whatsoever except as follows: _____; and

e. The balance of rental payments unpaid as of the date of this assignment is _____ Dollars ($_____), commencing with the next payment due on _____, 20__.

3.   Assignor understands and agrees that:

a. Assignee does not assume any of the obligations arising under the lease;

b. Assignor will keep and perform all of his obligations as lessor under the lease, and shall indemnify assignee against the consequences of any failure to do so;

c. Assignor will not assign any other interest in the lease, nor sell, transfer, mortgage, or encumber the property described in the lease, or any part thereof, without first obtaining the written consent of assignee;

d. Assignee may, at his discretion, give grace or indulgence in the collection of all rent and other sums due or to become due under the lease, and grant extensions of time for the payment of any such sums;

e. Assignor waives the right to require assignee to proceed against lessee, or to pursue any other remedy;

f. Assignor waives the right, if any, to obtain the benefit of or to direct the application of any security that is or may be deposited with assignee until all indebtedness of lessee to assignee arising under the lease has been paid; and

g. Assignee may proceed against assignor directly or independently of lessee, and the cessation of the liability of lessee for any reason other than full payment shall not in any way affects the liability of assignor hereunder, nor shall any extension, forbearance of acceptance, release, or substitution of security, or any impairment or suspension of assignee's remedies or rights against lessee in any way affect the liability of assignor hereunder.

4. Assignor guarantees due and punctual payment under the terms of the lease, and on any default by lessee, assignor will, on demand, repurchase the rights assigned hereunder by paying to assignee the then total unpaid balance of rental payments under the lease.

5. Assignor appoints assignee as his attorney in fact to demand, receive, and enforce payment and to give receipts, releases, and satisfactions and to sue for all sums payable, either in the name of assignor or in the name of assignee, with the same force and effect as assignor could have done if this assignment had not been made.

6. Notice of this assignment may be given at any time at assignee's option. In the event any payment under the lease hereby assigned is made to assignor, assignor will promptly transmit such payment to assignee.

7. This assignment is irrevocable and shall remain in full force and effect until and unless there is payment in full of any obligation, the payment of which is secured by it, or until and unless such obligation is released in writing by assignee.

Dated _____, 20___.

_____

ASSIGNMENT OF REAL ESTATE PURCHASE AND SALE AGREEMENT

THIS ASSIGNMENT is made this __ day of ____, 20__ by _____ (hereinafter referred to as "Assignor") to _____ (hereinafter referred to as "Assignee").

WITNESSETH:

WHEREAS, Assignor has entered into a certain Real Estate Purchase and Sale Agreement with ____ as "Seller" and Assignor as "Buyer" which Agreement was executed on _____, by said Assignor and on ____, by said Seller for the purchase and sale of certain real property being, lying and situate in _____ County, ____State, and more particularly described in said Agreement, copy of said Agreement being attached hereto as Exhibit "A"; and,

WHEREAS, Assignor desires to assign, transfer, sell and convey to Assignee all of Assignor's right, title and interest in, to and under said Real Estate Purchase and Sale Agreement; and,

WHEREAS, Assignee is desirous of receiving all of Assignor's right, title and interest in, to and under said Real Estate Purchase and Sale Agreement;

NOW, THEREFORE, for and in consideration of the sum of TEN DOLLARS ($10.00) and other good and valuable considerations, the receipt and sufficiency of which are hereby acknowledged, Assignor has assigned, transferred, sold and conveyed and by these presents does hereby assign, transfer, sell and convey unto Assignee all of Assignor's right, title and interest in, to and under said Real Estate Purchase and Sale Agreement.

Assignee hereby assumes all of Assignor's duties and obligations under said Real Estate Purchase and Sale Agreement.

This Assignment shall be binding upon Assignor and shall inure to the benefit of Assignee and its successors, heirs and assigns.

IN WITNESS WHEREOF this Assignment has been signed, sealed and delivered by Assignor and Assignee as of the day and year first above written.

Witnesses: "Assignor"

_____

_____

"Assignee"

_____

_____

MEMORANDUM OF CONTRACT FOR SALE AND PURCHASE OF PROPERTY

This is a Memorandum of that unrecorded Contract for Sale and Purchase of Property ("Contract"), dated _____, between _____, (hereinafter referred to as "Seller"), and _____, (herein after referred to as "Buyer") concerning the real property ("Property") described in Exhibit "A" attached hereto and made a part hereof by reference.

For good and valuable consideration, Seller has agreed to sell and Buyer has agreed to buy the Property upon the terms and conditions set forth in the Contract, which terms and conditions are incorporated in this Memorandum by this reference. Except as provided in the Contract from the date hereof, Seller shall not have the right, with respect to the Property to enter into any new contracts, leases or agreements, oral or written, without the prior written consent of Buyer.

This Memorandum is not a complete summary of the Contract. Provisions of this Memorandum shall not be used in interpreting the Contract. In the event of conflict between this Memorandum and the Contract, the Contract shall control.

IN WITNESS WHEREOF, the parties have executed this Memorandum on _____, 20__.

Witnesses: SELLER:

_____

_____

_____

_____

PURCHASER:

_____

_____

_____

_____

STATE OF _____) COUNTY OF _____) The foregoing instrument was acknowledged before me this ___ day of _____, 20___, by _____ as Seller.

_____ Notary Public

My Commission Expires: _____

STATE OF _____) COUNTY OF _____)

The foregoing instrument was acknowledged before me this ___ day of _____, 20___, by _____ as Purchaser.

_____ Notary Public

My Commission Expires: _____

MORTGAGE

THIS INDENTURE, made as of the ___ day of _____, 20___, by and between _____, of _____, hereinafter called "Mortgagor", and _____, of _____, hereinafter called "Mortgagee".

WITNESSETH:

AMOUNT OF LIEN: "NOTE"

WHEREAS, Mortgagor is justly indebted to Mortgagee in the sum of _____ DOLLARS ($_____) in lawful money of the United States, and has agreed to pay the same, with interest thereon, according to the terms of a certain note (the "Note") given by Mortgagor to Mortgagee, bearing even date herewith.

DESCRIPTION OF PROPERTY SUBJECT TO LIEN: "PREMISES".

NOW, THEREFORE, in consideration of the premises and the sum herein above set forth, and to secure the payment of the Secured Indebtedness as defined herein, Mortgagor has granted, bargained, sold and conveyed, and by these presents does grant, bargain, sell and convey unto Mortgagee property situate in _____ County, _____, more particularly described in Exhibit "A" attached hereto and by this reference made a part hereof; TOGETHER with all buildings, structures and other improvements now or hereafter located on, above or below the surface of the property herein before described, or any part and parcel thereof; and,

TOGETHER with all and singular the tenements, here determents, easements, riparian and littoral rights, and appurtenances thereunto belonging or in anywise appertaining, whether now owned or hereafter acquired by Mortgagor, and including all rights of ingress and egress to and from adjoining property (whether such rights now exist or subsequently arise) together with the reversion or reversions, remainder and remainders, rents, issues and profits thereof; and also all the estate, right, title, interest, claim and demand whatsoever of Mortgagor of, in and to the same and of, in and to every part and parcel thereof; and,

TOGETHER with all machinery, apparatus, equipment, fittings, fixtures, whether actually or constructively attached to said property and including all trade, domestic and ornamental fixtures, and articles of personal property of every kind and nature whatsoever (hereinafter collectively called "Equipment"), now or hereafter located in, upon or under said property or any part thereof and used or usable in connection with any present or future operation of said property and now owned or hereafter acquired by Mortgagor; and,

TOGETHER with all the common elements appurtenant to any parcel, unit or lot which is all or part of the Premises; and, ALL the foregoing encumbered by this Mortgage being collectively referred to herein as the "Premises";

TO HAVE AND TO HOLD the Premises hereby granted to the use, benefit and behalf of the Mortgagee, forever.

U.C.C. SECURITY AGREEMENT

It is agreed that if any of the property herein mortgaged is of a nature so that a security interest therein can be perfected under the Uniform Commercial Code, this instrument shall constitute a Security Agreement and Mortgagor agrees to join with the Mortgagee in the execution of any financing statements and to execute any and all other instruments that may be required for the perfection or renewal of such security interest under the Uniform Commercial Code.

EQUITY OF REDEMPTION

Conditioned, however, that if Mortgagor shall promptly pay or cause to be paid to Mortgagee, at its address listed in the Note, or at such other place which may hereafter be designated by Mortgagee, its or their successors or assigns, with interest, the principal sum of _____ DOLLARS ($_____) with final maturity, if not sooner paid, as stated in said Note unless amended or extended according to the terms of the Note executed by Mortgagor and payable to the order of Mortgagee, then these presents shall cease and be void, otherwise these presents shall remain in full force and effect.

ARTICLE ONE

COVENANTS OF MORTGAGOR

Mortgagor covenants and agrees with Mortgagee as follows:

1.01 Secured Indebtedness.

This Mortgage is given as security for the Note and also as security for any and all other sums, indebtedness, obligations and liabilities of any and every kind arising, under the Note or this Mortgage, as amended or modified or supplemented from time to time, and any and all renewals, modifications or extensions of any or all of the foregoing (all of which are collectively referred to herein as the "Secured Indebtedness"), the entire Secured Indebtedness being equally secured with and having the same priority as any amounts owed at the date hereof.

1.02 Performance of Note, Mortgage, Etc.

Mortgagor shall perform, observe and comply with all provisions hereof and of the Note and shall promptly pay, in lawful money of the United States of America, to Mortgagee the Secured Indebtedness with interest thereon as provided in the Note, this Mortgage and all other documents constituting the Secured Indebtedness.

1.03 Extent Of Payment Other Than Principal And Interest.

Mortgagor shall pay, when due and payable, (1) all taxes, assessments, general or special, and other charges levied on, or assessed, placed or made against the Premises, this instrument or the Secured Indebtedness or any interest of the Mortgagee in the Premises or the obligations secured hereby; (2) premiums on policies of fire and other hazard insurance covering the Premises, as required herein; (3) ground rents or other lease rentals; and (4) other sums related to the Premises or the indebtedness secured hereby, if any, payable by Mortgagor.

1.04 Insurance.

Mortgagor shall, at its sole cost and expense, keep the Premises insured against all hazards as is customary and reasonable for properties of similar type and nature located in_____ County, _____.

1.05 Care of Property.

Mortgagor shall maintain the Premises in good condition and repair and shall not commit or suffer any material waste to the Premises.

1.06 Prior Mortgage.

With regard to the Prior Mortgage, Mortgagor hereby agrees to:

(i) Pay promptly, when due, all installments of principal and interest and all other sums and charges made payable by the Prior Mortgage;

(ii) Promptly perform and observe all of the terms, covenants and conditions required to be performed and observed by Mortgagor under the Prior Mortgage, within the period provided in said Prior Mortgage;

(iii) Promptly notify Mortgagee of any default, or notice claiming any event of default by Mortgagor in the performance or observance of any term, covenant or condition to be performed or observed by Mortgagor under any such Prior Mortgage.

(iv) Mortgagor will not request nor will it accept any voluntary future advances under the Prior Mortgage without Mortgagee's prior written consent, which consent shall not be unreasonably withheld.

ARTICLE TWO

DEFAULTS

2.01 Event of Default.

The occurrence of any one of the following events which shall not be cured within _____ days after written notice of the occurrence of the event, if the default is monetary, or which shall not be cured within _____ days after written notice from Mortgagee, if the default is non-monetary, shall constitute an "Event of Default":

(a) Mortgagor fails to pay the Secured Indebtedness, or any part thereof, or the taxes, insurance and other charges, as herein before provided, when and as the same shall become due and payable;

(b) Any material warranty of Mortgagor herein contained, or contained in the Note, proves untrue or misleading in any material respect;

(c) Mortgagor materially fails to keep, observe, perform, carry out and execute the covenants, agreements, obligations and conditions set out in this Mortgage, or in the Note;

(d) Foreclosure proceedings (whether judicial or otherwise) are instituted on any mortgage or any lien of any kind secured by any portion of the Premises and affecting the priority of this Mortgage.

2.02 Options Of Mortgagee Upon Event Of Default.

Upon the occurrence of any Event of Default, the Mortgagee may immediately do any one or more of the following:

(a) Declare the total Secured Indebtedness, including without limitation all payments for taxes, assessments, insurance premiums, liens, costs, expenses and attorney's fees herein specified, without notice to Mortgagor (such notice being hereby expressly waived), to be due and collectible at once, by foreclosure or otherwise;

(b) Pursue any and all remedies available under the Uniform Commercial Code; it being hereby agreed that ten (10) days' notice as to the time, date and place of any proposed sale shall be reasonable;

(c) In the event that Mortgagee elects to accelerate the maturity of the Secured Indebtedness and declares the Secured Indebtedness to be due and payable in full at once as provided for in Paragraph 2.02(a) herein above, or as may be provided for in the Note, or any other provision or term of this Mortgage, then Mortgagee shall have the right to pursue all of Mortgagee's rights and remedies for the collection of such Secured Indebtedness, whether such rights and remedies are granted by this Mortgage, any other agreement, law, equity or otherwise, to include, without limitation, the institution of foreclosure proceedings against the Premises under the terms of this Mortgage and any applicable state or federal law.

ARTICLE THREE

MISCELLANEOUS PROVISIONS

3.01 Prior Liens.

Mortgagor shall keep the Premises free from all prior liens (except for those consented to by Mortgagee).

3.02 Notice, Demand and Request.

Every provision for notice and demand or request shall be deemed fulfilled by written notice and demand or request delivered in accordance with the provisions of the Note relating to notice.

3.03 Meaning of Words.

The words "Mortgagor" and "Mortgagee" whenever used herein shall include all individuals, corporations (and if a corporation, its officers, employees or agents), trusts and any and all other persons or entities, and the respective heirs, executors, administrators, legal representatives, successors and assigns of the parties hereto, and all those holding under either of them. The pronouns used herein shall include, when appropriate, both gender and both singular and plural. The word "Note" shall also include one or more notes and the grammatical construction of sentences shall conform thereto.

3.04 Severability.

If any provision of this Mortgage or any other Loan Document or the application thereof shall, for any reason and to any extent, be invalid or unenforceable, neither the remainder of the instrument in which such provision is contained, nor the application of the provision to other persons, entities or circumstances, nor any other instrument referred to herein above shall be affected thereby, but instead shall be enforced to the maximum extent permitted by law.

3.05 Governing Law.

The terms and provisions of this Mortgage are to be governed by the laws of the State of _____. No payment of interest or in the nature of interest for any debt secured in part by this Mortgage shall exceed the maximum amount permitted by law. Any payment in excess of the maximum amount shall be applied or disbursed as provided in the Note in regard to such amounts which are paid by the Mortgagor or received by the Mortgagee.

3.06 Descriptive Headings. The descriptive headings used herein are for convenience of reference only, and they are not intended to have any effect whatsoever in determining the rights or obligations of the Mortgagor or Mortgagee and they shall not be used in the interpretation or construction hereof.

3.07 Attorney's Fees.

As used in this Mortgage, attorneys' fees shall include, but not be limited to, fees incurred in all matters of collection and enforcement, construction and interpretation, before, during and after suit, trial, proceedings and appeals. Attorneys' fees shall also include hourly charges for paralegals, law clerks and other staff members operating under the supervision of an attorney.

3.08 Exculpation.

Notwithstanding anything contained herein to the contrary, the Note which this Mortgage secures is a non-recourse Note and such Note shall be enforced against Mortgagor only to the extent of Mortgagor's interest in the Premises as described herein and to the extent of Mortgagor's interest in any personality as may be described herein.]

IN WITNESS WHEREOF, the Mortgagor has caused this instrument to be duly executed as of the day and year first above written.

Witnesses: "Mortgagor" _____

Witnesses: "Mortgagee" _____

STATE OF _____) COUNTY OF _____)

THE FOREGOING instrument was acknowledged before me this _____ day of _____, 20___, by _____.

_____

My Commission Expires: _____

SECURITY DEPOSIT

Date Accepted: _____

Receipt is Hereby Acknowledged by _____ hereinafter Called Owner, From _____ hereinafter Called Resident, the sum of $_____ for the Security against default and damage of unit __ located at _____.

This deposit will be refunded to resident in the case that all conditions of the lease are met upon their departure.

_____

Owner Resident

OPTION AGREEMENT FOR PURCHASE
OF REAL PROPERTY

THIS OPTION AGREEMENT ("Agreement") made and entered into this ____ day of _____, 20___, by and between _____, whose principal address is _____, hereinafter referred to as "Seller" and _____, whose principal address is _____, hereinafter referred to as "Purchaser":

WITNESSETH:

WHEREAS, Seller is the fee simple owner of certain real property being, lying and situated in the County of _____, State of _____, such real property having the street address of _____ ("Premises") and such property being more particularly described as follows:

and,

WHEREAS, Purchaser desires to procure an option to purchase the Premises upon the terms and provisions as hereinafter set forth;

NOW, THEREFORE, for good and valuable consideration the receipt and sufficiency of which is hereby acknowledged by the parties hereto and for the mutual covenants contained herein, Seller and Purchaser hereby agree as follows:

1. DEFINITIONS. For the purposes of this Agreement, the following terms shall have the following meanings:

(a) "Execution Date" shall mean the day upon which the last party to this Agreement shall duly execute this Agreement;

(b) "Option Fee" shall mean the total sum of a down payment of _____ percent (___%) of the total purchase price of the Premises plus all closing costs, payable as set forth below;

(c) "Option Term" shall mean that period of time commencing on the Execution Date and ending on or before _____, 20___;

(d) "Option Exercise Date" shall mean that date, within the Option Term, upon which the Purchaser shall send its written notice to Seller exercising its Option to Purchase;

(e) "Closing Date" shall mean the last day of the closing term or such other date during the closing term selected by Purchaser.

2. GRANT OF OPTION. For and in consideration of the Option Fee payable to Seller as set forth herein, Seller does hereby grant to Purchaser the exclusive right and Option ("Option") to purchase the premises upon the terms and conditions as set forth herein.

3. PAYMENT OF OPTION FEE. Purchaser agrees to pay the Seller a down payment of _____ percent (_____ %) of the total purchase price of the Premises plus all closing costs upon the Execution Date.

4. EXERCISE OF OPTION. Purchaser may exercise its exclusive right to purchase the Premises pursuant to the Option, at any time during the Option Term, by giving written notice thereof to Seller. As provided for above, the date of sending of said notice shall be the Option Exercise Date. In the event the Purchaser does not exercise its exclusive right to purchase the Premises granted by the Option during the Option Term, Seller shall be entitled to retain the Option Fee, and this agreement shall become absolutely null and void and neither party hereto shall have any other liability, obligation or duty herein under or pursuant to this Agreement.

5. CONTRACT FOR PURCHASE & SALE OF REAL PROPERTY. In the event that the Purchaser exercises its exclusive Option as provided for in the preceding paragraph, Seller agrees to sell and Purchaser agrees to buy the Premises and both parties agree to execute a contract for such purchase and sale of the Premises in accordance with the following terms and conditions:

(a) Purchase Price. The purchase price for the Premises shall be the sum of _____ ($_____); however, Purchaser shall receive a credit toward such purchase price in the amount of the Option Fee thus, Purchaser shall pay to Seller at closing the sum of _____ ($_____);

(b) Closing Date. The closing date shall be on _____, 20_____ or at any other date during the Option Term as may be selected by Purchaser;

(c) Closing Costs. Purchaser's and Seller's costs of closing the Contract shall be borne by Purchase and shall be prepaid as a portion of the Option Fee;

(d) Default by Purchaser; Remedies of Seller. In the event Purchaser, after exercise of the Option, fails to proceed with the closing of the purchase of the Premises pursuant to the terms and provisions as contained herein and/or under the Contract, Seller shall be entitled to retain the Option Fee as liquidated damages and shall have no further recourse against Purchaser;

(e) Default by Seller; Remedies of Purchaser. In the event Seller fails to close the sale of the Premises pursuant to the terms and provisions of this Agreement and/or under the Contract, Purchaser shall be entitled to either sue for specific performance of the real estate purchase and sale contract or terminate such Contract and sue for money damages.

6. MISCELLANEOUS.

(a) Execution by Both Parties. This Agreement shall not become effective and binding until fully executed by both Purchaser and Seller.

(b) Notice. All notices, demands and/or consents provided for in this Agreement shall be in writing and shall be delivered to the parties hereto by hand or by United States Mail with postage pre-paid. Such notices shall be deemed to have been served on the date mailed, postage pre-paid. All such notices and communications shall be addressed to the Seller at _____ and to Purchaser at _____ or at such other address as either may specify to the other in writing.

(c) Fee Governing Law. This Agreement shall be governed by and construed in accordance with the laws of the State of _____.

(d) Successors and Assigns. This Agreement shall apply to, inure to the benefit of and be binding upon and enforceable against the parties hereto and their respective heirs, successors, and or assigns, to the extent as if specified at length throughout this Agreement.

(e) Time. Time is of the essence of this Agreement.

(f) Headings. The headings inserted at the beginning of each paragraph and/or subparagraph are for convenience of reference only and shall not limit or otherwise affect or be used in the construction of any terms or provisions hereof.

(g) Cost of this Agreement. Any cost and/or fees incurred by the Purchaser or Seller in executing this Agreement shall be borne by the respective party incurring such cost and/or fee.

(h) Entire Agreement. This Agreement contains all of the terms, promises, covenants, conditions and representations made or entered into by or between Seller and Purchaser and supersedes all prior discussions and agreements whether written or oral between Seller and Purchaser with respect to the Option and all other matters contained herein and constitutes the sole and entire agreement between Seller and Purchaser with respect thereto. This Agreement may not be modified or amended unless such amendment is set forth in writing and executed by both Seller and Purchaser with the formalities hereof.

IN WITNESS WHEREOF, the parties hereto have caused this Agreement to be executed under proper authority:

As to Purchaser this _____ day of _____, 20_____.

Witnesses: "Purchaser"

_____

_____

As to Seller this _____ day of _____, 20____.

Witnesses: "Seller" _____

QUIT CLAIM DEED

THE GRANTOR _____ of _____
City of _____, County of_____,
State of _____, for the consideration of _____
_____ CONVEY _____and QUIT
CLAIM_____ to _____ of _____,
City of_____, County of_____, State
of_____, all interest in the following described real estate in the
County of_____, in the State of_____, to wit:

Dated this____ day of_____,20___.

_____

Grantor's Signature

_____

Type or Print Name

_____

Recipient Signature

_____

Type or Print Name

_____

_____

STATE OF _____

COUNTY OF _____

I,_____, Notary Public in and for the
state of _____, do hereby certify that on this__
day of_____, 20__, personally appeared before me_____
known to be the individual described in and who executed the within instrument and acknowledged that _____ signed the
same as _____ free and voluntary act and deed for
the uses and purposes herein mentioned.

Given under my hand and official seal this___day of_____20___.
Commission expires_____20___.

_____
Notary Public

BALLOON MORTGAGE NOTE

$ _____

FOR VALUE RECEIVED, the undersigned, (jointly and severally, if more than one) promises to pay to _____, of _____, or order, in the manner hereinafter specified, the principal sum of _____ Dollars ($_____) with interest from date at the rate of _____ percent (_____%) per annum on the balance from time to time remaining unpaid. The said principal and interest shall be payable in lawful money of the United States of America at the address stated above, or at such place as may hereafter be designated by written notice from the holder to the maker hereof, on the date and in the manner following:

Principal and interest payments of $_____ each, due on or before the _____ day of each month, beginning _____, 20____, and continuing each month thereafter for a period of ____ years.

Then on _____, simultaneously with the payment of the _____ monthly payment, the full amount of unpaid principal, plus accumulated interest and any advances made, shall balloon and become immediately and fully due and payable, without demand.

This note with interest is secured by a mortgage on real estate, of even date herewith, made by the maker hereof in favor of the said payee, and shall be construed and enforced according to the laws of the State of _____. The terms of said mortgage are by this reference made a part hereof.

If default be made in the payment of any of the sums or interest mentioned herein or in said mortgage, or in the performance of any of the agreements contained herein or in said mortgage, then the entire principal sum and accrued interest shall at the option of the holder hereof become at once due and collectible without notice, time being of the essence; and said principal sum and accrued interest shall both bear interest from such time until paid at the highest rate allowable under the laws of the State of _____.

Failure to exercise this option shall not constitute a waiver of the right to exercise the same in the event of any subsequent default.

Each person liable hereon whether maker or endorser, hereby waives present-ment, protest, notice, notice of protest and notice of dishonor and agrees to pay all costs, including a reasonable attorney's fee, whether suit be brought or not, if, after maturity of this note or default hereunder, or under said mort-gage, counsel shall be employed to collect this note or to protect the security of said mortgage.

Whenever used herein the terms "holder", "maker" and "payee" shall be con-strued in the singular or plural as the context may require or admit.

"Maker" _____

"Holder" _____

ASSIGNMENT OF MORTGAGE

THIS ASSIGNMENT OF MORTGAGE (hereinafter referred to as the "Assignment") is made as of this _____ day of _____, 20 _____ by _____, whose address is _____ (hereinafter referred to as the "Assignor") for the benefit of _____, whose address is _____ (hereinafter referred to

WITNESSETH:

WHEREAS, Assignor is the holder of that certain Mortgage together with the debt and Note secured thereby, in the original principal sum of _____ Dollars ($_____)   given   by _____ as "Mortgagor", which Mortgage is recorded on the Public Records of _____ County, _____ at O.R. Book _____, Page _____ and which Mortgage encumbers and is a lien upon that certain real property described in Exhibit "A" attached hereto and by this reference made a part hereof (hereinafter referred to as the "Premises"); and,

WHEREAS, Assignor is desirous of assigning said Mortgage, together with the Note and the debt therein described, to Assignee; and

WHEREAS, Assignee is desirous of receiving and holding said Mortgage, together with the Note and the debt therein described, from Assignor.

NOW, THEREFORE, for and in consideration of the sum of _____ Dollars ($_____) paid by Assignee, and other good and valuable consideration, the receipt and sufficiency of which is hereby acknowledged by Assignor, Assignor does hereby make the following assignment:

1. Assignment. Assignor has granted, bargained, sold, assigned, conveyed and transferred, and by these presents does grant, bargain, sell, assign, convey and transfer unto Assignee, its heirs, successors and assigns, forever all of its right, title and interest in, to and under said Mortgage described above, together with the debt and Note secured thereby; together with any and all rights, interests and appurtenances thereto belonging; subject only to any right and equity of redemption of said Mortgagor, its successors or assigns in the same.

2. Warranties and Representations. Assignor hereby warrants and represents that it is the present holder of the above described Mortgage and that there are no other holders of said Mortgage or any interest therein nor is there any default by mortgagor therein or in the note and debt secured thereby.

3. Governing Law. This Assignment shall be governed, construed and interpreted by, through and under the laws of the State of _____.

4. Headings. Paragraph headings contained herein are for convenience of reference only and are not to be used in the construction or interpretation hereof.

IN WITNESS WHEREOF, Assignor has executed and delivered this Assignment to Assignee on the date hereof.

Witnesses: "Assignor" _____,

Witnesses: "Assignment"_____

STATE OF _____ COUNTY OF _____

THE FOREGOING instrument was acknowledged before me this ___ day of _____, 20__, by _____. _____ Notary Public

My Commission Expires: _____

BILL OF SALE

BILL OF SALE

STATE OF_____) ss: COUNTY OF _____)

KNOW YE ALL MEN BY THESE PRESENTS,

That, _____, of _____, for and in consideration of payment of the sum of $_____, the receipt of which is hereby acknowledged, do hereby grant, bargain, sell and convey to _____ of _____, and his heirs, executors, administrators, successors and assigns the following property as described below;

I hereby warrant that I am the lawful owner of said property and that I have full legal right, power and authority to sell said property. I further warrant said property to be free of all encumbrances and that I will warrant and defend said property hereby sold against any and all persons whomsoever.

IN WITNESS WHEREOF, I, the seller, have hereto set my hand and seal this ___day of _____, 20_____

STATE OF _____) ss: COUNTY OF _____)

On this __day of _____, 20___, before me personally came and appeared _____, known, and known to me, to be the individual described in and who executed the foregoing instrument, and who duly acknowledged to me that he executed same for the purpose therein contained.

IN WITNESS WHEREOF, I hereunto set my hand and official seal.

_____

My Commission Expires: _____

CONTRACT FOR PURCHASE AND SALE

This is a legally binding contract when signed by both parties. Consult a professional before signing if not fully understood!

PARTIES: _____, as "Seller" of _____, Phone: _____ and _____ as "Buyer" of _____, Phone: _____, hereby agree that the Seller shall sell and Buyer shall buy the

I. DESCRIPTION:

a) Legal description of real estate ("Property") located in _____ County, _____State.

b) Street address, if any, of the Property being conveyed is:

c) Personal property including all buildings and improvements on the property and all right, title and interest of Seller in and to adjacent streets, roads, alleys and rights-of-way, and:

II. PURCHASE PRICE to be paid by buyer for the above described property as follows;

PAYMENT:

a) Cash Deposit(s) to be held in escrow by _____ in the amount of $_____ and promissory note to be held in same escrow as additional earnest to show Buyer's intent in the amount of $_____

b) Subject to assumption of Mortgage in favor of _____ bearing interest at _____% per annum and payable as to principal and interest $_____ per month, having an approximate present principal balance of $_____, with _____ months left till end of terms.

c) Purchase money mortgage and note bearing interest at _____% on terms set forth herein below, in the principal amount of $_____, with payments of _____ per month for _____ months.

d) Other: _____ $_____

e) Other sum due seller at closing subject to adjustments and probations $_____

TOTAL PURCHASE PRICE $_____

f) All funds held in escrow shall be placed in an interest bearing account at the direction of Buyer, with interest accruing to the benefit of Buyer and either applied toward the purchase price at closing or returned to Buyer in the event and for any reason the transaction does not close.

g) Apportionment of Purchase Price and Deed; Land $_____ Main Structure $_____ Other $_____

III. FINANCING: If the purchase price or any part thereof is to be financed by a third party loan, this Contract for Sale and Purchase ("Contract"), is conditioned upon the Buyer obtaining a firm commitment for said loan within _____ days from the date hereof, at an interest rate not to exceed _____ percent (____%); of ____ years; and in the principal amount of $_____ _____. Buyer agrees to make application for, and to use reasonable diligence to obtain said loan. Should Buyer fail to obtain same or to waive Buyer's rights hereunder within said time, ___ Buyer may cancel Contract. ____Contract will continue under terms set forth on Addendum.

IV. TITLE EVIDENCE: Within twenty (20) days from the date of Contract, Seller shall, at his expense, deliver to Buyer or his attorney, in accordance with Paragraph XI, a title insurance commitment with fee owner's title policy premium to be paid by Seller at closing.

V. TIME FOR ACCEPTANCE AND EFFECTIVE DATE: If this offer is not executed by both of the parties hereto on or before _____, the aforesaid deposit(s) shall be, at the option of the Buyer, returned to him and this offer shall thereafter be null and void. The date of Contract ("Effective Date") shall be the date when the last one of the Seller and Buyer has signed this offer.

VI. CLOSING DATE: This transaction shall be closed and the deed and other closing papers delivered on the ____ day of _____, 20__, unless extended by other provisions of Contract, or by written agreement of the Parties.

VII. RESTRICTIONS, EASEMENTS, LIMITATIONS: The Buyer shall take title subject only to: Zoning, restrictions, prohibitions and other requirements imposed by governmental authority; Restrictions and matters appearing on the plat or otherwise common to the subdivision; Public utility easements of record; Taxes for year of closing and subsequent years, assumed mortgages and purchase money mortgages, if any; other: _____
provided, however, that none of the foregoing shall prevent use of the property for the purpose of _____.

VIII. OCCUPANCY: Seller represents that there are no parties in occupancy other than Seller, but if Property is intended to be rented or occupied beyond closing, the fact and terms thereof shall be stated herein, and the tenant(s) shall be disclosed pursuant to Paragraph XVII. Seller agrees to deliver occupancy of Property at time of closing unless otherwise specified below.

IX. ASSIGNABILITY: Buyer may assign this Contract.

X. TYPEWRITTEN OR HANDWRITTEN PROVISIONS: Typewritten or handwritten provisions inserted herein or attached hereto as Addenda shall control all printed provisions in conflict therewith.

XI. EVIDENCE OF TITLE: Within twenty (20) days from the date hereof, Seller, at Seller's sole cost and expense, shall cause a title insurance company mutually acceptable to the Parties ("Title Company") to issue and deliver to Buyer an ALTA Form B title commitment ("Title Commitment") accompanied by one copy of all documents affecting the Property, and which constitute exceptions to the Title Commitment. Buyer shall give Seller written notice on or before twenty (20) days from the date of receipt of the Title Commitment, if the condition of title as set forth in such Title Commitment and survey is not satisfactory in Buyer's sole discretion. In the event that the condition of title is not acceptable, Buyer shall state which exceptions to the Title Commitment are unacceptable. Seller shall, at its sole cost and expense promptly undertake and use its best efforts to eliminate or modify all unacceptable matters to the reasonable satisfaction of Buyer. In the event Seller is unable with the exercise of due diligence to satisfy said objections within thirty (30) days after said notice, Buyer may, at its option: (i) extend the time period for Seller to satisfy said objections, (ii) accept title subject to the objections raised by Buyer, without an adjustment in the purchase price, in which event said objections shall be deemed to be waived for all purposes, or (iii) rescind this Agreement, whereupon the deposit described herein shall be returned to Buyer and this Agreement shall be of no further force and effect.

XII. EXISTING MORTGAGES TO BE ASSUMED: Seller shall furnish to Buyer within twenty (20) days from execution hereof a statement from all mortgagee(s) setting forth principal balance, method of payment, interest rate and whether the mortgage(s) is in good standing. If a mortgage requires approval of the Buyer by the mortgagee in order to avoid default, or for assumption by the Buyer of said mortgage, and:

a) the mortgagee does not approve the Buyer, the Buyer may rescind the contract, or

b) the mortgagee requires an increase in the interest rate or charges a fee for any reason in excess of $500.00, the Buyer may rescind the Contract unless Seller elects to pay such increase or excess. Seller and Buyer each shall pay 50% of any such fee. Buyer shall use reasonable diligence to obtain approval. The amount of any escrow deposits held by mortgagee shall be credited to Seller.

XIII. PURCHASE MONEY MORTGAGES: The purchase money note and mortgage, if any, shall provide for a thirty (30) day grace period in the event of default if it is a first mortgage and a 15 day grace period in the event of default if a second mortgage; shall provide for right of prepayment in whole or in part without penalty; shall be assumable and shall not provide for acceleration or interest adjustment in event of resale of the Property. Said mortgage shall require the owner of the encumbered Property to keep all prior liens and encumbrances in good standing.

XIV. CURRENT SURVEY: Within fifteen (15) days from the date hereof, Seller, at Seller's sole cost and expense, shall furnish a current survey of the Property prepared and certified by a duly registered Land Surveyor. The survey as to the Property shall:

a) Set forth an accurate legal description; and

b) Locate all existing easements and rights-of-way (setting forth the book and page number of the recorded instruments creating the same), alleys, streets, and

c) Show any encroachments; and

d) Show all existing improvements (such as buildings, power lines, fences, etc.); and

e) Show all dedicated public streets provided access and whether such access is paved to the property line; and

f) Show the location of any easements necessary for the furnishing of off-site improvements; and

g) Be certified to the Seller, the Buyer, the Title Company and any lender that may be involved in the transaction.

In the event the survey or the recertification thereof shows any encroachments of any improvements upon, from, or onto the Property, or on or between any building set-back line, a property line, or any easement, except those acceptable to Buyer, in Buyer's sole discretion, said encroachment shall be treated in the same manner as a title defect under the procedure set forth of notice thereof with

XV. TERMITES: The Buyer, within time allowed for delivery of evidence of title and examination thereof, or no later than ten (10) days prior to closing, whichever date occurs last, may have the improvements inspected at ___Buyer's ___Seller's expense by a certified pest control operator to determine whether there is any visible active termite infestation or visible existing damage from termite infestation in the improvements. If Buyer is informed of either or both of the foregoing, Buyer will have ten (10) days from date of notice thereof within which to have all damages, whether visible or not, inspected and estimated by a licensed building or general contractor. Seller shall pay valid costs for treatment and repair of all damage up to 1 1/2% of Purchase Price. Should such costs exceed that amount, Buyer shall have the option of canceling contract within five (5) days after receipt of contractor's repair estimate by giving written notice to Seller, or Buyer may elect to proceed with the transaction, in which event Buyer shall receive a credit at closing of an amount equal to 1 1/2% of said Purchase Price. "Termites" shall be deemed to include all wood destroying organisms.

XVI. INGRESS AND EGRESS: Seller warrants that there is ingress and egress to the Property sufficient for the intended use as described in Paragraph VII hereof the title to which is in accordance with Paragraph XI above.

XVII. LEASES: Seller shall, not less than fifteen (15) days prior to closing, furnish to Buyer copies of all written leases and estoppel letters from each tenant (if any) specifying the nature and duration of said tenant's occupancy, rental rates and advanced rent and security deposits paid by tenant. In the event Seller is unable to obtain such letter from each tenant, the same information shall be furnished by Seller to Buyer within said time period in the form of a Seller's affidavit, and Buyer may thereafter contact tenants to confirm such information. Seller shall deliver and assign all original leases to Buyer at closing.

XVIII. LIENS: Seller shall, both as to the Property and personality being sold hereunder, furnish to Buyer at time of closing an affidavit attesting to the absence, unless otherwise provided for herein, of any financing statements, claims of lien or potential lienors known to Seller and further attesting that there have been no improvements to the Property for ninety (90) days immediately preceding date of closing. If the property has been improved within said time, Seller shall deliver releases or waivers of all mechanic's liens, executed by general contractors, subcontractors, suppliers, and material men, in addition to Seller's lien affidavit setting forth the names of all such general contractors, subcontractors, suppliers and material men and further reciting that, in fact, all bills for work to the Property which could serve as a basis for a mechanic's lien have been paid or will be paid at closing.

XIX. PLACE OF CLOSING: Closing shall be held in the county wherein the Property is located, at the office of the attorney or other closing agent designated by Buyer; provided, however, that if a portion of the purchase price is to be derived from an institutional mortgagee, the requirements of said mortgagee as to time of day, place and procedures for closing, and for disbursement of mortgage process, shall control, anything in this contract to the contrary notwithstanding.

XX. TIME: Time is of the essence of this Contract. Any reference herein to time periods of less than six (6) days shall in the computation thereof, exclude Saturdays, Sundays and legal holidays, and any time period provided for herein which shall end on a Saturday, Sunday or legal holiday shall extend to 5:00 p.m. of the next business day.

XXI. DOCUMENTS FOR CLOSING: Seller shall furnish deed, closing statement, mechanic's lien affidavit, assignments of leases, and any corrective instruments that may be required in connection with perfecting the title.

Buyer shall furnish mortgage, mortgage note, security agreement, and financing statement.

XXII.EXPENSES: State documentary stamps which are required to be affixed to the instrument of conveyance, intangible tax on and recording of purchase money mortgage to Seller, and cost of recording any corrective instruments shall be paid by Seller. Documentary stamps to be affixed to the note or notes secured by the purchase money mortgage, cost of recording the deed and financing statements shall be paid by Buyer.

If needed an appraisal shall be done at the expense of the ___ Buyer ___ Seller.

Any repairs required by FHA or VA shall be at the expense of the ___ Buyer ___Seller.

Any other inspections required by law will be at the expense of the ___ Buyer ___Seller.

XXIII. PRORATION OF TAXES: Taxes for the year of the closing shall be prorated to the date of closing. If the closing shall occur before the tax rate is fixed for the then current year, the apportionment of taxes shall be upon the basis of the tax rate of the preceding year applied to the latest assessed valuation. Subsequent to the closing, when the tax rate is fixed for the year in which the closing occurs, Seller and Buyer agree to adjust the proration of taxes and, if necessary, to refund or pay, as the case may be, an amount necessary to effect such adjustments. This provision shall survive closing.

XXIV. PERSONAL PROPERTY INSPECTION, REPAIR: Seller warrants that all major appliances, heating, cooling, electrical, plumbing systems, and machinery are in working condition as of six (6) days prior to closing. Buyer may, at his expense, have inspections made of said items by licensed persons dealing in the repair and maintenance thereof, and shall report in writing to Seller such items as found not in working condition prior to taking of possession thereof, or six (6) days prior to closing, whichever is first. Unless Buyer reports failures within said period, he shall be deemed to have waived Seller's warranty as to failures not reported. Valid reported failures shall be corrected at Seller's cost with funds therefore escrowed at closing. Seller agrees to provide access for inspection upon reasonable notice.

XXV. RISK OF LOSS: If the improvements are damaged by fire or other casualty prior to closing, and the costs of restoring same does not exceed 3% of the assessed valuation of the improvements so damaged, cost of restoration shall be an obligation of the Seller and closing shall proceed pursuant to the terms of Contract with costs therefore escrowed at closing. In the event the cost of repair or restoration exceeds 3% of the assessed valuation of the improvements so damaged, Buyer shall have the option of either taking the Property as is, together with either the said 3% or any insurance proceeds payable by virtue of such loss or damage, or of canceling the Contract and receiving return of deposit(s) made hereunder.

XXVI. MAINTENANCE: Notwithstanding the provisions of Paragraph XXIV, between Effective Date and Closing Date, all personal property on the premises and real property, including lawn, shrubbery and pool, if any, shall be maintained by Seller in the condition they existed as of Effective Date, ordinary wear and tear excepted, and Buyer or Buyer's designee will be permitted access for inspection prior to closing in order to confirm compliance with this standard.

XXVII. PROCEEDS OF SALE AND CLOSING PROCEDURE: The deed shall be recorded upon clearance of funds and evidence of title continued at Buyer's expense, to show title in Buyer, without any encumbrances or change which would render Seller's title unmarketable from the date of the last evidence, and the cash proceeds of sale shall be held in escrow by Seller's attorney or by such other escrow agent as may be mutually agreed upon for a period of not longer than five (5) days from and after closing date. If Seller's title is rendered unmarketable, Buyer shall within said five (5) day period, notify Seller in writing of the defect and Seller shall have thirty (30) days from date of receipt of such notification to cure said defect. In the event Seller fails to timely cure said defect, all monies paid hereunder shall, upon written demand therefore and within five (5) days thereafter, be returned to Buyer and, simultaneously with such repayment, Buyer shall vacate the Property and reconvey same to the Seller by special warranty deed. In the event Buyer fails to make timely demand for refund, he shall take title as is, waiving all rights against Seller as to such intervening defect except as may be available to Buyer by virtue of warranties, if any, contained in deed.

XXVIII. ESCROW: Any escrow agent receiving funds is authorized and agrees by acceptance thereof to promptly deposit and to hold same in escrow and to disburse same subject to clearance thereof in accordance with terms and conditions of Contract. Failure of clearance of funds shall not excuse performance by the Buyer.

XXIX. ATTORNEY FEES AND COSTS: In connection with any litigation including appellate proceedings arising out of this Contract, the prevailing party shall be entitled to recover reasonable attorney's fees and costs.

XXX. (a) DEFAULT BY SELLER: In the event that Seller should fail to consummate the transaction contemplated herein for any reason, except Buyer's default; (i) Buyer may enforce specific performance of this Agreement in a court of competent jurisdiction and in such action shall have the right to recover damages suffered by Buyer by reason of the delay in the acquisition of the Property, or (ii) may bring suit for damages for breach of this Agreement, in which event, the deposit made hereunder shall be forthwith returned to Buyer, or (iii) declare a default, demand and receive the return of the deposit. All rights, powers, options or remedies afforded to Buyer either hereunder or by law shall be cumulative and not alternative and the exercise of one right, power, option or remedy shall not bar other rights, powers, options or remedies allowed herein or by law.

XXX. (b) DEFAULT BY BUYER: In the event Buyer should fail to consummate the transaction contemplated herein for any reason, except default by Seller or the failure of Seller to satisfy any of the conditions to Buyer's obligations, as set forth herein, Seller shall be entitled to retain the earnest money deposit, such sum being agreed upon as liquidated damages for the failure of Buyer to perform the duties and obligations imposed upon it by the terms and provisions of this Agreement and because of the difficulty, inconvenience and uncertainty of ascertaining actual damages, and no other damages, rights or remedies shall in any case be collectible, enforceable or available to Seller other than as provided in this Section, and Seller agrees to accept and take said deposit as Seller's total damages and relief hereunder in such event.

XXXI. MEMORANDUM OF CONTRACT RECORDABLE, PERSONS BOUND AND NOTICE: Upon the expiration of the inspection period described in paragraph XXXVI, if Buyer has elected to proceed with purchase of the property, the parties shall cause to be recorded, at Buyer's option and expense, in the public records of the county in which the property is located, an executed Memorandum of Contract as attached hereto. This Contract shall bind and inure to the benefit of the Parties hereto and their successors in interest. Whenever the context permits, singular shall include plural and one gender shall include all. Notice given by or to the attorney for either party shall be as effective as if given by or to said party.

XXXII. PRORATIONS AND INSURANCE: Taxes, assessments, rent, interest, insurance and other expenses and revenue of the Property shall be prorated as of date of closing. Buyer shall have the option of taking over any existing policies of insurance on the Property, if assumable, in which event premiums shall be prorated. The cash at closing shall be increased or decreased as may be required by said prorations. All references in Contract to prorations as of date of closing will be deemed "date of occupancy" if occupancy occurs prior to closing, unless otherwise provided for herein.

XXXIII. CONVEYANCE: Seller shall convey title to the Property by statutory warranty deed subject only to matters contained in Paragraph VII hereof and those otherwise accepted by Buyer. Personal property shall, at the request of Buyer, be conveyed by an absolute bill of sale with warranty of title, subject to such liens as may be otherwise provided for herein.

XXXIV. UTILITIES: Seller shall, at no expense to Seller, actively work with Buyer to assist Buyer in obtaining electricity, water, sewage, storm drainage, and other utility services for development of the Property.

a) Seller will transfer all utility deposits where possible to Buyer upon closing? ___ Yes ___ No

XXXV. ENGINEERING PLANS AND STUDIES: Upon the execution hereof, Seller shall furnish to Buyer all engineering plans, drawings, surveys, artist's renderings and economic and financial studies which Seller has, if any, relating to the Property, and all such information may be used by Buyer in such manner as it desires; provided that in the event Buyer fails to purchase the Property for any reason other than Seller's default, all such information shall be returned to Seller together with any information that Purchaser may have compiled with respect to the Property.

XXXVI. INSPECTION OF PROPERTY: Buyer shall have sixty (60) days from the date hereof to determine the elevation, grade, and topography of the Property and to conduct engineering and soil boring tests as the Buyer deems necessary in order to determine the usability of the Property. Buyer may in its sole and absolute discretion, give notice of termination of this Agreement at any time prior to the expiration of the sixty (60) day inspection period, and upon such termination, all deposits held in escrow shall be returned to Buyer.

XXXVII. PENDING LITIGATION: Seller warrants and represents that there are no legal actions, suits or other legal or administrative proceedings, including cases, pending or threatened or similar proceedings affecting the Property or any portion thereof, nor has Seller knowledge that any such action is presently contemplated which might or does affect the conveyance contemplated hereunder.

XXXVIII. SURVIVAL OF REPRESENTATIONS AND WARRANTIES: The representations and warranties set forth in this Contract shall be continuing and shall be true and correct on and as of the closing date with the same force and effect as if made at that time, and all of such representations and warranties shall survive the closing and shall not be affected by any investigation, verification or approval by any party hereto or by anyone on behalf of any party hereto.

XXXIX. ACQUIRING APPROVALS: The obligation of Buyer to close is conditioned upon Buyer's having acquired all the necessary approvals and permits to use the property for_____.

XL. OTHER AGREEMENTS: No prior or present agreements or representations shall be binding upon any of the Parties hereto unless incorporated in this Contract. No modification or change in this Contract shall be valid or binding upon the Parties unless in writing, executed by the Parties to be bound thereby.

XLI. SPECIAL CLAUSES:

_____

_____

_____

Witnesses: Executed by Buyer on: _____

_____ Buyer

_____

_____ Buyer

_____

Executed by Seller on: _____

_____ Seller

_____

_____ Seller

_____

Deposit(s) under II (a) received; if check, subject to clearance, and terms hereof are accepted.

By:_____ (Escrow Agent)

BROKERAGE FEE: ___Seller ___Buyer agrees to pay the registered real estate Broker named below compensation in the total amount of _____ percent (_____%) of gross purchase price of $_____ for his services in accordance to the contract in affect between the two parties.

_____ Broker Seller

_____ Seller

_____ Buyer

About the Author

The author, Ron Searcy, was born in Southern-Middle Tennessee in 1945.

He married in 1965 and in 1968, served in the US Army and attained the rank of sergeant within the minimum fifteen months required time.

After getting out of the Army in 1970, by accident he wound up in the construction business, specializing in, insurance claims repair.

About the time that he went into business for himself, he was lead to read a book called, "See You At The Top" by Zig Ziglar and this book absolutely changed his life. Within nine years from the time he read that book he became a self-made millionaire.

Having moved to Chattanooga, Tennessee in 1970 where, he got into the construction business, he bought a 348 acre farm and moved back to his home town in 1977.

In 1982, he received some junk mail and responded to it because of the unusual name of the book. The book tried to persuade the reader that anyone could write books and that, there were more self-made millionaires in the self publishing business than anything else in America.

Though it has not been published to date, he wrote his first book in 1983 which, was a manual on the insurance claims repair business.

In 1992, while working as a storm adjuster during hurricane Andrew, he was led to write his first book, "Divorced In The Courthouse, But Not In Heaven". This book was finally published in 2000.

Mr. Searcy attended the Chattanooga school of teaching and preaching in 1984 with the idea not being a preacher but, to obtain further knowledge. He spent five years studying with different religious groups with the idea of trying to find out what different groups' doctrinal views were and why they believed it. His purpose was to find the true church that you read about in the New Testament. His latest book, "How Anyone Can Understand The Bible," is due out in the fall of 2005.

Mr. Searcy has been an entrepreneur for thirty years and has experience in several different fields therefore, he is knowledgeable in many fields and has another book titled "From Bankruptsy To A Millionaire—Twice—A true Story", coming out shortly following this books' release.

"From Bankruptcy To A Millionaire—Twice: A True Story," is a true story about his life and the unbelievable things that happened to him and how he was able to overcome those things that would have destroyed most people.

You may order any of Mr. Searcy's works by e-mailing at musiccitypress@aol.com and get on a first list basis when the books mentioned are printed and are ready to go in the next couple of months.

978-0-595-42743-7
0-595-42743-X

www.ingramcontent.com/pod-product-compliance
Lightning Source LLC
Chambersburg PA
CBHW031054180526
45163CB00002BA/830